Cooking on the Coast

The O'Keefe Family Recipe Book

COMPILATION AND RESEARCH
Rose Annette O'Keefe

PRODUCTION AND EDITING
Joseph Saxon O'Keefe

Library of Congress Catalog Card Number pending.
ISBN Number: 0-9641501-0-7
Cover design and original artwork by Joseph S. O'Keefe

First Printing - June 1994
Second Printing - November 1994

For additional copies contact:
Cooking on the Coast
P.O. Box 430
Ocean Springs, MS 39566-0430

Printed in the USA by

WIMMER
The Wimmer Companies, Inc.
Memphis • Dallas

Gracious Lord, you hear and answer our prayers.
Let your light shine on all who have given their talents to this book,
And bless all who prepare the recipes herein.
Nourish us with your love and the food from your bounty,
And we thank you for the family and friends you have so
generously provided.

Amen.

Introduction

January 11, 1994

Biloxi, Mississippi, for many years, has charmed and attracted people the world over to its inviting shores. Named for the tribe of Biloxi Indians who were its first known inhabitants, many artifacts have been discovered buried near magnificent oak trees that grace the waterfront. Most of these artifacts pertained to cooking and truly spark one's thoughts as to what it must have been like. It's easy to imagine these primitive people choosing the hillsites and the most beautiful pieces of land on which to build their dwellings and hold council meetings.

As time passed, European explorers came here to claim the land and dwell thereon. This brought an influx of different nationalities that comprise the population of Biloxi's people today. It also provided the many advantages of ethnic cultures, which in turn affected the types of foods and cooking enjoyed here.

Being right on the Gulf of Mexico where fish, shrimp and oysters abound, one has the benefit of very fresh seafood. At one time Biloxi was the only city in the country that canned shrimp and oysters. Many families from Yugoslavia came to fish these waters and, in time, Vietnamese families followed. Both of these have distinctive recipes and food preparations, and they opened restaurants soon after arriving in Biloxi. Along with Greek, Spanish, French,

German, Italian and Mexican cuisines, dating from earlier immigration to the Mississippi Gulf Coast, we have seafood restaurants deluxe, as well as the ever popular "po' boy" places.

The Biloxi Lighthouse, which dates back to 1848 and the pre-Civil War era, is not only a landmark along coastal Highway 90, it is still a functioning beacon, sending out its rays to boats unequipped with radar. It is open to the public once a year during the Spring Garden Pilgrimage. Reportedly, it was painted black at the time of President Lincoln's assassination, portraying the mourning of our nation.

Biloxi has become a tourist mecca and is noted everywhere today for the colorful gambling casinos nestled along its shoreline with the promise of more to come. The east end of town, known to locals as "The Point" has been transformed from a center of the seafood industry into a playground and amusement park with a Vegas-like atmosphere.

Biloxi beckons more than ever to persons searching for fun, good food and the lure of lady luck. Maybe you will visit us some day?

The O'Keefe Family

My husband has always said, "510 Beach Boulevard is where the action is." To house, raise, educate and feed a family of 13 children has been a challenge, a joy and lots of work.

The children are grown, educated and gone from the homeplace, but Mom and Dad O'Keefe are still in the cooking business. Each Sunday, when possible, Mom gathers all the available clan, and Dad, in his own inimitable way, fries eight to ten chickens. Or, he may do a tremendous pot of chicken-sausage gumbo. The girls help with the salad, always making homemade dressing, while son Jeff does the rolls.

O'Keefe Family (c. 1965 ?)
(back row from left) Susan, Virginia, Kathryn, Cecilia, Maureen, Jody, Jim
(front row from left) Mary, Justin, Mercedes, Dad, Mom, Joe, John, Jeff.

For many years Mrs. Teresa O'Keefe, Dad's mother, provided dozens of cupcakes, plain and frosted, for dessert. "Nannaw", as she is known, has reached the venerable age of 99 years and still comes to the family meal after attending Mass.

So, with this background in mind, we hope you will see how this cookbook evolved, as each individual from this family went forth, to return with unusual and tempting dishes.

Please enjoy our recipes, or just reading how a big family made it work.

Rose Annette Saxon O'Keefe

Childhood Memories of Kathryn O'Keefe

When I heard that Joe, the youngest in our family of 13 children, was requesting that the family send in its favorite recipes for a family cookbook, memories began flooding my mind. It seems amazing to me that we have all inherited, or acquired through the years, a talent and love of cooking and sharing with family and friends. Although we have always had an abundance of food, there was very little variety in the weekly menu during our younger years.

I suppose Moma and our housekeeper, Florence Pettis, were too busy with 13 children to make changes in the weekly menus at the family table, which usually went as follows: Red Beans and Rice on Mondays—Meatballs and Spaghetti on Tuesdays—Chuck Roast with Potatoes, Onions and Carrots on Wednesday—Leftovers or Fricasseed Chicken on Thursdays—Fried fish or Courtbouillon on Fridays. I also recall a number of Friday nights that we had Franco-American Hot Tamales and Pork-and-Beans, which we liked as well. That was the "quick and easy" meal we had when Mom and Dad had plans to go out on Friday nights. On Saturdays at noon, we usually had hamburgers and french fries. In our early years, Moma made homemade pizza for us on Saturday night. In later years, when there were quite a few more of us, we all had "steak" on Saturday night, which meant that the children had hot dogs early in the evening and Mom and Dad would have a Sirloin Steak with Bleu Cheese melted on it. There was usually enough for us to have a taste of that too, when we were persistent enough.

Florence cooked Fried Chicken for us every Sunday morning. She started cooking early in the morning and we would awake to the wonderful aroma of fresh, hot fried chicken. When I entered the kitchen, Florence would be standing before the large frying pans, constantly poking and turning each piece of chicken to keep them from burning. I usually sat at the kitchen table and visited with her for awhile and shortly would comment on how good the chicken smelled, inquiring if a small piece was done that I might nibble.

*That approach was usually
rewarded with a taste of the
best fried chicken you could
imagine. My brothers were
more blunt; they usually
wandered in and went
straight to the oven where
the cooked chicken was
being carefully guarded by
Florence. They would wait
until she was distracted
and try to grab a choice
piece of chicken, resulting
in a poke of the frying fork
on their hands and a loud
exclamation from her of
"Anhhh!" or "Gon-don-
it!"*—*her version of "Dog-gone-it!" After Florence passed away,
Dad took over frying chicken duty and seems to thoroughly enjoy
it, even though it's a tremendous amount of work to cut up nine or
more chickens, individually salt and pepper each piece, dust it in
flour and fry it. Instead of having to stand guard over the chicken
to make sure there is enough to get to the table, he always cooks
extra so that anyone who wants a taste or two before lunch can
comfortably do so without admonition.*

*Florence Pettis, (c. 1978) a beloved part of
the O'Keefe family for well over three decades.*

*As the years have passed the menu has become diversified with
dishes such as Seafood Gumbo, Crawfish Bisque or Dad's Chicken
Gumbo and many other delicious creations. These are now
specialties of the house that have replaced most of the old repetitious
weekly menus that kept 13 children well-fed and satisfied.*

Kathryn O'Keefe

Author's Acknowledgements and Appreciations

To my husband, Jerry O'Keefe, to all of our children, relatives and friends, I want to say "thank you" for your encouragement, patience and your contributions to helping me see a dream come true. More than a year ago, our youngest son Joe said, "Moma, it's time to write the cookbook you've been promising all your life." As a matter of fact, I had tried on two previous occasions to do this very thing, and was interrupted by Hurricane Camille and later, multiple reasons.

Joe, now working at Foreign Affairs magazine in New York City, had at his disposal lots of sophisticated equipment. He offered to do all the production and design work, if I could pull together the recipes and photos. I contacted the family through my weekly newsletter, telling them of the proposed venture, and asked them for recipes, anecdotes, pictures and a name for "the book."

Through many phone calls, letters and family gab sessions, which produced lots of funny memories (like the time our schnauzer ate the cake we had put away for dessert), we have finally put together what I hope will be an interesting and desirable cookbook containing some of our best recipes. The kitchen has always been the place in our home where we gather and "where the action is." The recipes are tried, true and tested many times over, evolving into the "specialties" that are the mark of good cooks. Most of these have been done by our children—a group of discerning brothers and sisters who think they are as good, or better, in the kitchen than Mom and Dad ever were. I think they all deserve chef's bonnets and neckerchiefs.

I would be remiss not to mention the majordomos who helped to shepherd our family over a period of forty-something years. These wonderful women were part of the family and helped raise the children, did a lot of the cooking and managed our home. They were Florence Pettis, our housekeeper who came to temporarily "help out" and stayed for 30 years. Her successor was Corita Johnson, who came to "give Florence a hand" in her last days and stayed for an additional 12 years. And now, Ruby Taylor has come to continue following Corita's retirement. It is impossible to estimate the impact these ladies have had on our family as they wove their way into our hearts and lives. You will find many of their special recipes in the book.

You will find informational excerpts as those making contributions come alive to you through their recipes. My wish is that you will go beyond this book and enjoy making your own creations using what we have put together for you, that you will enjoy getting to know the O'Keefes on a culinary basis, and that you will come to know the charms of the Mississippi Gulf Coast.

Rose Annette O'Keefe

Table of Contents

The O'Keefe Family (c. 1990)
(back row, from left) Susan, Jim, Mary, Maureen, Mom, Jeff, Dad,
Cecilia, Virginia, Kathryn, Jody; *(front row, from left)* Justin, Joe, Mercedes, John.

SALADS, SALAD DRESSINGS & SAUCES

SOUPS AND SIDE DISHES

SEAFOOD

ENTREES---BEEF, PORK & GAME

ENTREES--POULTRY

MISCELLANEOUS ENTREES

DESSERTS, SWEETS & BREADS

APPETIZERS

*"It's hard to imagine that 50 years have passed since we spoke our vows
in the Ranch House Chapel of Camp Pendleton, California. I remember the day
so clearly. I wore a shell pink silk jersey two-piece outfit. My hat was a soft
green straw that came forward and was topped with two huge shell pink
Malmaison roses of silk. My corsage was of giant gardenias and the fragrance
still brings back memories of that day. Dad of course wore his Marine Corps
uniform and looked so handsome. We were so young . . . I asked my mother and
Mrs. O'Keefe to stand as matrons of honor so neither would have to be left alone
during the ceremony. Would I ever have dreamed of being a parent to so many
children? You know the answer to that one. I was scared enough as it was. God,
of course, knew exactly what He was doing."*

Rose Annette O'Keefe

Ripe Olive Dip

2 cans ripe olives, minced   3 tablespoons olive oil
2 tomatoes, minced   1½ tablespoons wine vinegar
2 green onions, minced   1 teaspoon garlic salt
Jalapeno peppers to taste   Dash of Tabasco

Combine vegetable ingredients, place in a large bowl and then stir in olive oil, wine vinegar, garlic salt and Tabasco. Chill for at least one hour. Serve with tortilla chips.

Virginia O'Keefe Brown

Giant Taco

2 cans black olives
1 bunch of green onions
2 medium tomatoes
1 cup jalapeno peppers
2 cans refried beans
1 16-ounce container, sour cream
1 package dry taco mix
1 8-ounce Cheddar cheese (shredded)
Paprika

Chop black olives, green onions, tomatoes and jalapeno peppers. Shred cheddar cheese. Using a large plate, pan or platter, first layer the refried beans, olives, onions and tomatoes. Mix sour cream, dry taco mix and (if courageous) add about two tablespoons of jalapeno juice. Then add the Cheddar cheese and sprinkle with paprika. You may sprinkle with Tony Chachere's seasoning too, if available.

Virginia O'Keefe Brown

Scrumptious Sour Cream Dip

2 16-ounce containers of sour cream
1 can pitted ripe olives, chopped
2 packages of Hidden Valley Party Dip (dry mixture)
1 cup jalapeno peppers, chopped
3 tablespoons jalapeno juice
2 tablespoons Cavender's Greek seasoning
½ teaspoon of cayenne pepper

Stir all ingredients together and chill. If it is too spicy, cut back on the jalapeno portions or cayenne.

Virginia O'Keefe Brown

Mary's Italian Olives

1 quart large green olives (*with seeds in*)

2 teaspoons marjoram	3 green onions,minced
2 teaspoons oregano	¼ cup capers
2 teaspoons basil	½ cup vinegar
1 teaspoons salt	¼ cup wine vinegar
Juice of 2 lemons	½ cup olive oil

Pour mixture over olives after bruising each olive. Marinate for 24 hours. Invert occasionally. Use liquid for salad dressing and add a little more lemon to reduce calories. (To "bruise" olive, use a wooden mallet and give olive a whack on one side.)

Mary O'Keefe Sumrall

Crab Appetizer

8 ounces fresh lump crabmeat
1 small yellow onion, minced
3 tablespoons fresh parsley, minced
11 ounces cream cheese, softened
2 tablespoons mayonnaise
6 ounces chili sauce or picante sauce
1 tablespoon lemon juice
2 tablespoons Worcestershire sauce
½ teaspoon garlic salt

Combine cream cheese, onion, mayonnaise, lemon juice, garlic salt and Worcestershire sauce. Spread on serving plate. Second layer is chili or picante sauce. Top layer is crabmeat. Sprinkle parsley on top of crabmeat. Serve with melba toast rounds or crackers.

Susan O'Keefe Snyder

Marinated Shrimp

10 pounds shrimp
2 medium onions, quartered
3 tomatoes, quartered
1 bell pepper, sliced

4 stalks celery, chopped
1 pound fresh mushrooms
1 medium can black olives

Marinade:
3 bay leaves
1 cup white vinegar
Juice of 5 lemons
½ cup Lea & Perrins
2 cups salad oil

3 tablespoons garlic, finely minced
2 tablespoons salad herbs
1 teaspoon salt
1 cup parsley

Peel shrimp and boil until pink. Combine shrimp and vegetables in a large container. Combine marinade ingredients and pour over shrimp and vegetables. Cover container and chill for at least four hours. Serves 30.

Chris Snyder

Smoked Fish

Fresh fish, preferably fillet
2 quarts water
1 cup non-iodized salt
½ cup brown sugar
2 tablespoons lemon concentrate
1 tablespoon garlic powder
¼ tablespoon onion powder

Combine all ingredients except fish to make brine. Soak fish in brine 4 or more hours. Rinse and dry on paper towels. Smoke at 70-80 degrees until done over hickory chips. Six hours if the fish is split; 12 hours if whole.

John Michael O'Keefe

Shrimp Mold

2 pounds chopped, boiled shrimp
1½ cans tomato soup
1 8-ounce package Philadelphia Cream Cheese
1 cup chopped celery, minced fine
1 cup chopped onions, minced fine
1 cup mayonnaise
4 packages Knox Gelatin, dissolved in 1 cup hot water
Horseradish
Hot sauce
Red pepper
Salt

Boil tomato soup. Add cream cheese, blend until smooth. Add celery, onions, mayonnaise, shrimp and gelatin/water. Mix all together very well (so your mold will be smooth). Grease bundt pan very well. Season it to your taste, the more red pepper, salt, hot sauce and horseradish you put in it, the better it tastes. Let it set in the refrigerator over night.

Barbara Neustrom

Shrimp Dip/Spread

4 cups boiled, seasoned shrimp, peeled and diced finely
½ cup celery, minced   3 tablespoons lemon juice
½ cup stuffed olives   2 cloves garlic, pressed
½ cup sweet pickles, diced   1 cup mayonnaise
½ cup green onions, chopped   2 packs cream cheese, softened
⅓ cup bell pepper, diced   Tony Chachere's seasoning

Mix shrimp, celery, olives, pickles, onions and bell pepper. Blend remaining ingredients in blender until smooth. Combine shrimp mixture and cream sauce until well blended. Season to taste. Chill and serve with Ritz crackers.

Cecilia O'Keefe Neustrom

Oysters Rockefeller

4 dozen oysters   1 can mashed anchovies
1 bunch green spinach   Salt to taste
2 bunches green onions   Louisiana hot sauce
1 stalk celery   2 ounces anisette liqueur
1 bunch parsley   ¾ cup Parmesan cheese
1 pound butter, melted   ¾ cup bread crumbs
1½ cup bread crumbs   4 dozen oyster shells
3 tablespoons Lea & Perrins   1 box rock salt

Chop spinach, onion, celery and parsley in a food processor until very fine. Mix in 1 pound butter, melted, and 1½ cups bread crumbs. Season with Lea & Perrins sauce, mashed anchovies, salt and hot sauce to taste. Sauté oysters in skillet for a few minutes until juice comes forth and edges curl. Then put oysters in shells, place shells on rock salt, and cover each with some sauce. Cover with cheese and additional bread crumbs. Bake in 450-degree oven until brown. Serve hot, accompanied by freshly sliced wedges of lemon (*optional*). Yields enough for 4 entrees. Note: Sauce may be frozen, but do not add anisette liqueur until sauce is thawed and ready to spread on oysters.

Rose Annette O'Keefe

Eggplant Oyster Appetizers

2 medium eggplants (6 cups diced)
1 pint fresh shucked oysters
½ cup oyster liquid
3 tablespoons butter
¾ cups chopped onions
½ teaspoon crushed garlic
½ cup diced bell peppers
2 tablespoons flour
¼ cup half and half
3 tablespoons minced green onions
2 tablespoons minced parsley
1 tablespoon Worcestershire sauce
¼ teaspoon cayenne pepper
¼ teaspoon black pepper
½ teaspoon salt
Points of bread toasted or patty shells
½ cup bread crumbs
½ cup Parmesan cheese
½ cup grated sharp cheese
½ teaspoon Italian herbs

Peel and dice eggplant, steam in a little water until tender, drain and set aside. In a saucepan heat oysters, in their own juices, until the edges begin to curl (3-4 minutes). Drain and reserve liquid. Melt butter in a sauté pan, add onions, garlic, and bell pepper and cook until just transparent, add flour, stir until well blended, add oyster liquid and half and half. Cook until thick and smooth. Add green onions and parsley, stir well. Add eggplant and coarsely chopped oysters (or whole if very small). Add seasonings, herbs and grated cheese, stir well and cool slightly. Spread on toast points or fill patty shells. Combine bread crumbs and Parmesan cheese, sprinkle on each appetizer. Bake in 350-degree oven about 12-15 minutes or until brown on top. Serve warm or at room temperature. Yields 36-40 appetizers.

Lorelei Stroble

Oysters Bienville

1 pound cooked, deveined shrimp, chopped
2 dozen oysters on the half shell, liquid drained just before preparation
1 medium onion, minced
½ stick butter
3 tablespoons flour
½ pint half & half
½ cup dry white wine
1 cup chicken stock or bouillon
1 small carton sliced mushrooms
Unseasoned bread crumbs
Grated Romano & Provolone cheese

Sauté the onion in the butter until tender. Add the flour, cook about 1 minute, stirring. Gradually add the half & half, stirring each time until well blended and it begins to thicken again. Do not let it come to a boil. Repeat with the wine, then the stock, you may need a little more or less stock than called for, if more you can substitute wine or milk, etc. Adjust seasoning with salt and pepper.

Add the shrimp and mushrooms, consistency may have to be adjusted after adding the shrimp. You want to finish with a sauce that is medium thick.

Drain and place oysters in their shells, place filled shells in a bed of rock salt on a cookie sheet. Bake at 325 degrees about 5 minutes. Use tongs and drain each oyster again, replace shells on rock salt. Spoon the sauce over each oyster, lightly sprinkle some bread crumbs and cheese over each and bake at 350 degrees until golden brown.

Jerry "Jody" O'Keefe, Jr.

Some people extract the juice from the oysters by sautéeing them in a skillet for a few minutes before putting the oysters in shells.
Rose Annette O'Keefe

Oysters Italiano

3 dozen oysters, liquid reserved
1 small white onion, chopped
3 cloves garlic chopped
½ cup olive oil
4 slices bacon chopped
3 slices proscuitto or ham, chopped
1 rib celery
1 large bell pepper, chopped
1 cup dry white wine
½ pound butter, softened
2 egg yolks
2 cups unseasoned Italian bread crumbs
½ cup grated Romano cheese
1 teaspoon oregano
1 tablespoon basil
Juice of 1 large lemon
Lea & Perrins Worcestershire sauce
Salt, black, white & red pepper to taste

Sauté onion and garlic in olive oil until tender. Add bacon, ham, celery, bell pepper and sauté until tender. Continue cooking over medium high until bacon begins to crisp. Add wine, oyster liquid and cook until reduced by one third. Correct seasonings. Pour vegetable mixture into a food processor and add all remaining ingredients (except oysters). Process until pureed and well mixed.

Preheat oven to 450 degrees. Place oysters in small dishes or on their shells. Place sauce on each oyster and bake until golden brown.

Jerry "Jody" O'Keefe, Jr.

Aunt Mary's Minced Oysters

1 quart oysters
1 bunch green onions, minced
1 bunch parsley, minced
1 stick butter
2 teaspoons salt
2 teapoons black pepper
1 tablespoon Worcestershire sauce
1 medium-sized dill pickle, minced
Juice of 1 lemon
¼ pound salted crackers

Sauté onions and parsley in butter. Drain oysters, saving juice to use later if needed. Mince oysters, using two sharp knives. Add oysters to sauteed onion and parsley, stir until juice is well blended. Thicken mixture with crushed crackers and turn off heat. Season to taste with salt, pepper, Worcestershire, minced dill pickle and lemon juice.

Prepare as a casserole with cracker crumbs and dotted with butter. Heat at 350 degrees in oven until bubbly hot. May also be served as a cocktail dip, in a chafing dish with Ritz crackers; or, as an entree in clam shells accompanied with a salad and hot rolls; or, as a fancy hors d'oeuvre, using the minced oyster mix as a stuffing in puff pastry shells.

Mary Cahill O'Keefe

This family recipe began with Aunt Mary, who taught me how to prepare it. I, in turn, have passed it on to my son-in-law, Chris Snyder, who does the honors for family banquets. This recipe is supremely good and always a hit.

Rose Annette O'Keefe

Sicilian Oysters

4 dozen oysters and liquid
1 large onion, chopped
2 cloves garlic, finely chopped
 (or 1 teaspoon powder)
1 stick butter
2 tablespoons parsley, chopped
1 lemon, cut in wedges

½ teaspoon red pepper
½ teaspoon thyme
¾ teaspoon oregano
Tony Chachere's to taste
1 cup seasoned bread crumbs
¼ cup Parmesan cheese

Saute onions in butter; add seasoning; add oysters. When edges curl, add liquid from oysters. Fold in 1 cup bread crumbs. Put in casserole or individual dishes, sprinkle with Parmesan cheese. Bake at 350 degrees for 15-20 minutes. Serve with lemon wedges.

Kathryn O'Keefe

Mild Uncooked Salsa

6 medium tomatoes, diced
2 medium onions, chopped
1 small bell pepper, diced
2-4 ounces diced green chili peppers
1 tablespoon chili powder
1 6-ounce can pitted black olives, sliced
1 teaspoon sugar
¼ cup chopped fresh cilantro
1 teaspoon black pepper
(or 2 tablespoons dried crushed coriander)
Jalapeno peppers to taste
1½ teaspoon garlic salt

½ cup oil
⅓ cup vinegar
⅓ cup lemon juice

Combine all ingredients, seasonings and blend. Pour into airtight container and chill overnight. Serve uncooked with tortilla chips. Will keep for a week if kept refrigerated.

Mary O'Keefe Sumrall

Hot Salsa

4 large onions
1 large carrot
2 fresh tomatoes
4-5 doz. fresh green hot pepper
(the long skinny variety--not jalapenos)

2 cans crushed tomatoes
½ - ¾ cup cider vinegar
Salt to taste

Chop onions, carrot, peppers and fresh tomatoes in processor. Bring to a boil with crushed tomatoes, cider vinegar and salt. Simmer for one hour. If too hot or too thick, thin with V-8 juice, tomato juice, ketchup or tomato sauce.

If you like a medium or mild hot sauce, de-seed the peppers. If using a food processor to chop, the seeds have a tendency to stick to the top of the bowl. They can be easily scooped out and discarded.

Kathryn O'Keefe

Corita's Salsa

17 cans of chopped tomatoes
4 cups of chopped onions
2 cups chopped bell pepper
1 large ground carrot
25 marinated jalapeno peppers
(1 ½ cups chopped)
⅔ cups cider vinegar
1 tablespoon salt
⅓ cup of sugar

Mrs. Corita Johnson

Grind first five ingredients in food processor. Put in a large pot (16-quart size), then add remaining ingredients and bring to a boil. Simmer for one hour, adjust seasonings to taste, and simmer for another hour. Pour into clear jars, and apply lids after salsa has cooled to near room temperature.

Corita Johnson

Corita Johnson worked for the O'Keefe family for 12 years, bringing more to the task than one could have asked. To our family, she has been a close friend, counselor and confidante—not to mention a great cook—through good years and bad. Although retired now, she remains a cherished part of our extended family and her gumbo, stuffed crabs, salsa and cakes are still in demand.

Rose Annette O'Keefe

Ceci Saxon's Pimento Cheese Dip

2 blocks medium or sharp Cheddar cheese , grated
1 medium-sized jar chopped pimentos
1-2 bunches green onions, chopped
1 bunch fresh parsley, chopped
2 tablespoons jalapeno peppers, chopped
1-2 large cooking spoons jalapeno juice
        (approx. 3 tablespoons)
2 cups mayonnaise
Cavender's Seasoning to taste
Green Olives, chopped (*optional*)

Mix all ingredients together.

Virginia O'Keefe Brown

*This recipe has been handed down for three generations. Each time
it varies a little. In the original version, sweet pickle relish was
used. Then jalapenos were added in next version. Now, jalapenos
and Cavender's are used. I still like to use all the options.*

Rose Annette O'Keefe

Cheese Krisps

2 cups Rice Krispies
2 sticks oleo
2 cups grated NY sharp cheese
2 cups flour

½ teaspoon salt
¼ teaspoon cayenne

Blend oleo and cheese. Sift flour, salt and cayenne pepper.
Mix with butter & cheese mixture. Add Rice Krispies. Shape
into tiny balls. Flatten on ungreased cookie sheet (press
down with fork). Bake 15 minutes at 350 degrees. Makes
about 60.

Nicki C. O'Keefe

Quick Party Cheese Ball

½ pound Velveeta cheese
4 ounces cream cheese
1 cup pecans, chopped

1 teaspoon red pepper
1 teaspoon garlic powder
Dash of chili powder

Combine above ingredients. Shape into a ball. Use pecans to coat outside of ball or mix with cheese if preferred.

Mary O'Keefe Sumrall

Debra's Beefy Cheese Balls

16 ounces cream cheese, softened
2 cups pecans, chopped
3 to 4 green onions, chopped
2 jars dried beef (minced)

Reserve one fourth minced beef and combine above ingredients. Shape into ball. Then use one fourth of minced dried beef to coat outside of ball.

Mary O'Keefe Sumrall

Pineapple-Cheese Ball

16 ounces cream cheese, softened
8 ounces crushed pineapple, thoroughly drained
2 tablespoons chopped green onions
¼ cup finely chopped green pepper
1 cup of chopped pecans
1 tablespoon seasoned salt

Combine cream cheese, pineapple, pepper, onion, and salt; mix well. Chill. Form mixture into a ball, and roll it in pecans. Yield: 15 servings.

Susan O'Keefe Snyder

Swell Cheese Straws

⅓ cup grated cheddar cheese 4 tablespoons flour
1 tablespoon butter ½ cup fresh bread crumbs
1½ tablespoon milk 1 teaspoon cayenne pepper

Cream cheese and butter. Add milk. Mix in flour and bread crumbs and season. Knead until smooth. Roll, then cut in strips and bake in oven at 400 degrees.

Carolyn B. Sasser

Moma's Pickled Okra

1 pound fresh okra
2 cloves garlic ½ cup salt
1 teaspoon dill seed 4 cups vinegar
2 hot peppers 1 cup water

Pack trimmed okra upright in 1 quart jar. Add garlic, peppers, and dill seed. Bring water, vinegar, and salt to a boil and pour over okra. Add more of boiled mixture if initial pouring soaks down. Seal jar. Yield: 1 quart.

Rose Annette O'Keefe

Pickled Eggs

4 to 5 dozen eggs, boiled & peeled
½ gallon distilled white vinegar
1 cup water
½ cup salt
½ box of pickling spice
Juice from 16-ounce can beets

Combine in a large pot the vinegar, water and salt. Bring to a boil. Add pickling spice. Add juice from can of beets. Put peeled eggs in a large jar or container, then pour mixture over eggs.

Rose Annette O'Keefe

Sweet and Sour Pickles

6 large sour pickles, sliced
2 cups sugar
Dash of celery seeds

3 cloves of garlic, sliced
12 cloves

Combine ingredients and let sit for three days, stirring mixture once or twice. Wash jars in dish washer, fill with mixture and then seal jars. You may also want to add a bit more sugar and some of the liquid from the sour pickles (e.g. 6 cups of sugar for 1 gallon of pickles).

Celia Saxon Carron

These pickles are as sweet as my sweet sister.

Rose Annette O'Keefe

Artichoke Squares

12 ounces marinated artichokes
1 onion, chopped
1 clove garlic, minced
4 eggs
¼ cup bread crumbs

Dash of Tabasco
½ teaspoon oregano
½ teaspoon salt
½ teaspoon pepper
2 cups cheddar cheese
(*shredded*)

Drain juice of one 6-ounce jar of artichokes into skillet. Saute onion and garlic. Drain the other 6-ounce jar, set aside. Chop artichokes. In a bowl beat eggs. Add bread crumbs, Tabasco, oregano, salt and pepper. Stir in artichoke mixture, then add cheese. Mix well. Bake in 9 X 13" pan for 30 minutes at 325 degrees. Cut into squares and serve hot. Can be made in advance and rewarmed. Makes about 30 squares.

Note: Swiss Cheese may be substituted for part of Cheddar. For thicker squares, use 7 X 11" pan.

Mary O'Keefe Sumrall

Artichoke Toast

1 6-ounce jar marinated artichokes
1 cup mayonnaise
2 ounces Parmesan cheese, grated
3 ounces Romano cheese, grated
2 green onions, minced
Louisiana hot sauce to taste
Melba toast or cocktail toast rounds or crackers

Mix all ingredients and spread on the toast. Bake at 350 degrees until bubbly. *Jerry "Jody" O'Keefe, Jr.*

Bruschetta

5-6 ripe tomatoes
1 loaf French bread
Fresh basil, chopped

1 cup olive oil
2-3 cloves garlic
Salt

Rub crust of bread with garlic. Slice loaf into ¾ in slices. Place bread flat on a cookie sheet and toast lightly. Dice tomatoes and add ½ cup fresh chopped basil, stir. Remove bread from oven and top each slice with ¾ cup of tomato/basil mixture. Return to oven at 450 degrees and roast until tips of tomatoes begin to turn brown. Sprinkle olive oil and salt over each. Garnish with basil leaf. *Sam Ward*

Eggplant Sandwiches

1 eggplant
Salt water
8 ounces cream cheese, softened
1 tablespoon olive oil

Dash Tabasco sauce
2 eggs beaten with water
2 cups bread crumbs

Peel eggplant and cut into thin slices. Dip in salt water, dry and spread each slice with softened cheese mashed and mixed with olive oil and dash of Tabasco sauce. Pair slices like sandwiches and allow to stand several minutes to blend flavors. Dip in egg, crumbs and fry in pan lightly coated with oil or butter. *Caroline B. Sasser*

Steamed Artichokes

4 large artichokes
3 lemons, sliced thin
Paprika

4 tablespoons Tony Chachere's
seasoning

Wash artichokes and remove stems. Sprinkle with Tony Chachere, garnish with lemon slices and paprika. Then steam in covered pot 45 minutes or until leaves can be easily pulled loose. Serve with lemon, butter dip or a sauce of oil, wine vinegar and Romano cheese. Note: If no Tony Chachere is available, a mixture of 2 tablespoons salt, 2 tablespoons black pepper, 2 tablespoons cayenne pepper, 2 tablespoons garlic powder and paprika may be used.

Rose Annette O'Keefe

Stuffed Artichokes

4 large artichokes
2 cups Romano cheese
1 cup dried parsley
4 cups Italian bread crumbs
12 garlic cloves, minced

4 slices lemon
Paprika
Salt
Pepper
1 cup olive oil

Mix bread crumbs, cheese, garlic, parsley, salt and pepper. Slice off tops and bottoms of artichokes, spread leaves open. Stuff mixture in each leaf, place the artichokes in a pot, then pour olive oil over them. Steam in pot with tight lid, using enough water to last perhaps 45 minutes to 1 hour. When leaves come off easily, they are ready to serve.

Rose Annette O'Keefe

Pizza Rounds

1 pound hot sausage
1 pound ground beef
½ teaspoon Worcestershire
½ teaspoons garlic salt

1 pound Velveeta cheese
1 teaspoon oregano
Sliced olives for topping
2 loaves of party rye

Brown sausage and beef together in skillet. Drain off all grease. Add cubed Velveeta cheese to meats, and stir until cheese is thoroughly melted. Remove skillet from heat and add Worcestershire sauce, garlic salt and oregano. Spread mixture onto party rye bread, topping each slice with sliced green olives. Place bread on a cookie sheet and bake at 400 degrees for 15 minutes.

Susan O'Keefe Snyder

Green Olive Mix

1 10-ounce jar sliced salad olives with pimentos, drained
1 10-ounce large pimento stuffed olives drained, half coarsely chopped, half whole
2 bunches green onions, minced
1 cup Greek salad peppers, minced
1 4¼-ounce can sliced black olives, drained
⅓ cup capers, drained
½ cup celery, minced
½ cup fresh cauliflower, minced
1 carrot, minced
2 cloves garlic, minced
1½ teaspoon basil
1 tablespoon parsley, fresh or dried
1 large bottle of Italian salad dressing
½ cup cider vinegar

In large bowl, combine ingredients and mix well. Transfer to air-tight container and refrigerate. Can be used as a salad dressing or muffelata dressing. Adding juice of 1 lemon is optional. Refrigerate after each use. *Mary O'Keefe Sumrall*

Vegetable Dip

8 ounces sour cream   ⅓ small bottle of dill weed
8 ounces mayonnaise   Few shakes garlic powder
3 tablespooons minced onion

Combine all ingredients and refrigerate for at least 1 hour.
Use with fresh vegetables for appetizer.

Tabouli I

1 cup warm water   Salt and pepper
2 cups cracked wheat or bulgur   ½ to 1 cup olive oil
1 cup chopped parsley   1 cup lemon juice
½ cup chopped onions   2 tablespoons fresh mint
2 tomatoes, chopped   (or 1 of dried mint)

Soak wheat in water for one hour. Then combine with
remaining ingredients and serve with crackers.

Rose Annette O'Keefe

Tabouli II

4 cups boiling water   ¾ cup fresh mint
1¼ cups bulgur wheat   ¾ cup green onion
¼ cup dry white beans   ½ tablespoon salt
 (*cooked and mashed*)   ¼ cup olive oil
3 medium tomatoes   ½ cup lemon juice
1½ cups minced parsley   Pepper to taste

Soak wheat in water for two hours. Combine bulgur, beans,
parsley, mint, onions, tomatoes, lemon juice, olive oil, salt
and pepper. Serve with crackers.

May substitute garbanzo beans for white beans.

Rose Annette O'Keefe

Mary O'Keefe Sumrall and Ron Sumrall in the O'Keefe kitchen in Biloxi.

Natchez Caviar

3 16-ounce cans Trappey's jalapeno black-eyed peas, drained
1 8-ounce bottle Italian dressing
1½ cups chopped onion
1 cup chopped green onions
½ cup chopped jalapeno peppers
2 cups chopped green peppers
1 4-ounce jar chopped pimento, drained

Mix all ingredients. Let stand in refrigerator 8 hours prior to serving. Serve as a dip with taco chips.

I place all ingredients in a zip-lock bag and turn occasionally to marinate. I also substitute greek salad peppers for part of the chopped jalapeno. This way it isn't so hot.

Mary O'Keefe Sumrall

King's Hawaiian Party Dip

1 package Leek soup mix
1 package frozen, chopped spinach
    (thawed & drained, but not cooked).
1 cup mayonnaise
1 cup sour cream
Dash of Worcestershire sauce
1 8-ounce can chopped water chestnuts or shrimp

Mix together all ingredients. For best results in flavor, mix dip the day before or at least 8 hours before using and refrigerate. To serve, hollow out round boat of bread, reserving the crust. Tear bread center into bite-sized pieces and surround loaf. Fill bread center with Hawaiian dip.

Annette Longeway O'Keefe

Ceviche

2 fish fillets, cut into cubes (Amber, king, snapper)
½ pound peeled deveined medium shrimp
    Optional: scallops or conch if available
1 medium onion, coarsely chopped
1 large tomato, peeled & chopped
2 cloves garlic, minced
¼ bunch finely chopped parsley
¼ cup fresh lime juice
¼ cup fresh lemon juice
½ cup olive oil
½ cup tomato juice
Dash of thyme
Salt & black pepper to taste
2-3 chili peppers, minced (*optional*)

Combine all ingredients. Correct seasonings. Cover and refrigerate overnight. Serve cold in small cups with a fork or toothpick.

Jerry "Jody" O'Keefe, Jr.

Beef Jerky I

Chuck roast, sliced thin

1¼ cups sugar
¼ cup salt
2 cups soy sauce
½ cup water
1 cup red wine

Lots of Tabasco
1 tablespoon garlic powder
1½ tablespoons black pepper
1 tablespoon onion powder

While chuck roast is still partially frozen, put slices in marinade above and marinate overnight in refrigerator. Smoke until done over hickory chips (approximately 10-12 hours).

Beef Jerky II

1 to 2 pounds flank steak
½ cup soy sauce

Garlic salt to taste
Lemon pepper to taste

Cut steak with the grain in long strips no more than ¼ inch thick. Combine meat and soy sauce; toss to coat evenly. Drain and discard soy sauce. Sprinkle both sides of strips lightly with seasonings. Place strips in a single layer on an ungreased cookie sheet. Bake at 150 degrees for 10 hours (do not allow temperature to go over 150 degrees). Yield: ¼ to ½ pound of jerky. Note: Partially freeze meat for easy slicing. Store jerky in air-tight container.

SALADS, DRESSINGS & SAUCES

Cecile B. Saxon, known as "Moma Ceci," a beautiful woman of French-Canadian descent and the mother of Rose Annette O'Keefe. She used to feed peanut butter-and-jelly sandwiches to the squirrels on the back steps of her house in Ocean Springs, Mississippi. In later years, her sister, Caro, kept a BB-gun handy on the back porch in case the neighborhood cats tried to steal the morsels. Ceci loved to garden, keep house, and cook special things. She always welcomed visitors to her lovely home, entertaining them in the sun room.

Moma's Crab Salad

This is a lovely recipe for a ladies luncheon or shower. Light, yet filling.

2 heads curly lettuce
1 dozen eggs, hard boiled
6-7 pounds fresh lump crabmeat
6 sticks celery, finely minced
3 cups mayonnaise
3 lemons, juice of
2 tablespoons curry powder
Paprika
Radishes
Green olives
Black olives
Egg halves

Prepare lettuce—wash and crisp in refrigerator. Mince six of the eggs, add to crabmeat with minced celery. Make a dressing of mayonnaise, lemon juice and curry powder. Toss with crabmeat mixture being careful not to overmix or break up lump crabmeat. Make a bed of lettuce on each salad plate, put 1½ cups salad in center. Garnish with radishes, olives, eggs and paprika. Serve with dainty rolls and crackers. Allow ½ pound crabmeat per person for generous helping. Serves 12 to 14.

Rose Annette O'Keefe

Caesar Salad

2 heads Romaine lettuce
2 cloves garlic, mashed
1 can anchovy filets, mashed
½ cup olive oil
1 egg, coddled (soft boiled)
2 lemons, juice of
Dash of Worcestershire
Dash of red pepper
3 tablespoons Parmesan cheese
2 cups toasted croutons

Wash, tear into bite sized pieces, and crisp lettuce in refrigerator. In large wooden bowl mash garlic and anchovies in olive oil. Add egg, lemon juice, Worcestershire sauce and red pepper. Mix well. Place lettuce into bowl with dressing, toss lightly, sprinkle with Parmesan cheese and serve with croutons. To make croutons, sprinkle cubed bread with olive oil, Parmesan cheese and brown in oven. Important to serve salad as soon as prepared.

Rose Annette O'Keefe

Marinated Seafood Salad

This recipe was inspired by a dish of Mercedes Hall, Ocean Springs, Mississippi; she and her husband, Leon, are among the very dearest of my parent's friends. This has never failed to woo the crowd! At a buffet, it is always the first dish to get gobbled up!

Munchies:
4 pounds jumbo shrimp, cooked , peeled & deveined
2 pounds blue-crab claw fingers (must be fresh for this dish)
2 white onions, quartered & separated
1 bunch celery, cut into bite size pieces
4 large bell peppers, cut into bite size strips
2 cartons cherry tomatoes
2 cans pitted whole black olives
3 16-ounce cartons fresh mushrooms
2 12-ounce cans artichoke hearts, quartered
1 bunch large fresh asparagus
2 bunches green onions, washed & trimmed
1 12-ounce can large green olives unpitted - crushed lightly with a mallet

Marinade:
1 large bottle Wishbone Italian Dressing
1½ cups olive oil
1 cup red wine vinegar
1 cup cider vinegar
5 bay leaves
1 bunch parsley, minced
¼ cup Lea & Perrins Worcestershire sauce
1 clove garlic, chopped
3 tablespoons paprika
2 tablespoons black pepper
2 tablespoons basil
2 teaspoons oregano
1 teaspoon thyme
1 teaspoon cayenne pepper

continued on next page

Seafood Salad (cont'd)

Preparation:
Heat a pot of salted water to boiling, add shrimp and turn heat to medium low. Do not let the pot come back to a boil, let shrimp steep in the very hot water until pink and firm (3 - 4 minutes max), remove pot from heat, drain hot water and rinse in cold water until shrimp are cold. Drain water, cover and refrigerate.

Steam or boil asparagus with lightly salted water until they are just "al dente" (still slightly crunchy). In an appropriate size (large enough to hold the munchies and marinade) serving vessel of your choice, (flatter is prettier) place the shrimp and all other munchies except the crab claw fingers.

Mix marinade ingredients in a bowl and pour over munchies, toss, stir, or mix very well. Add crab claw fingers and mix in very gently - they will shred apart if mistreated. Cover with plastic wrap, refrigerate at least 4 hours or overnight, lifting bottom munchies to the top 4 or more times.

Jerry "Jody" O'Keefe, Jr.

Spaghetti Salad

1 medium package vermicelli, cooked in mixture of water and canned chicken broth
1 small jar green stuffed olives, drained and sliced
2 medium tomatoes, chopped   1 jar chopped artichoke hearts
1 large cucumber, chopped   1 can pitted black olives, sliced
1 cup fresh broccoli, chopped   1 jar Italian salad dressing
½ jar Salad Toppings by McCormick
Salt, pepper and red pepper to taste

Combine above ingredients and chill. Light and refreshing on a hot summer evening. Try adding chopped shrimp and substituting other vegetables for variation.

Cecilia O'Keefe Neustrom

Pasta Shrimp Salad

2 bags Rotini pasta
2 pounds shrimp, peeled & deveined
Salt and Tony Chachere's seasoning, to taste

2 large red onions, chopped
2 heads broccoli florets
½ head cauliflower florets
4 stalks celery, sliced and chopped
1 sweet bell pepper, chopped
1 cup minced pimento
3 cups small stuffed green olives (or black pitted olives)
3 cups marinated artichokes
1 cup jalapenos, minced

1 tablespoon dried basil
2 teaspoons dried tarragon
1 cup wine vinegar
1 cup cider vinegar
1 cup lemon juice, fresh
Grated lemon rind of one lemon
1 tablespoon garlic powder
2 tablespoons paprika
4 cups olive oil

Boil pasta al dente (chewy) in salted water. Drain in colander then pour 1 cup olive oil over to keep from sticking. Steam peeled shrimp in 1 cup water seasoned with Tony Chachere's. Put aside both pasta and shrimp. Prepare the next nine ingredients, put in very large salad bowl.

Use last nine ingredients to make marinade. Combine everything, then let sit at room temperature to blend all ingredients. With hot garlic bread this recipe will make a great lunch. Shrimp may be omitted if not available, or if all-vegetable salad is preferred. Serves 18-20.

Rose Annette O'Keefe

Shrimp Diavolo Salad or Dip

1 pound small fresh shrimp
3 hard boiled eggs
1 26-ounce jar Newman's Own Bandito Diavolo sauce
½ cup Creole mustard (coarsely ground brown mustard)
¼ cup olive oil
½ cup cider vinegar
1 (2¼ ounces) can sliced black olives
3 green onions
1 head lettuce
1 lemon or lime

Peel shrimp and place in 2 quart pot. Add 2 cups water and bring to boil. Boil for one minute and drain water. Put boiled shrimp in large mixing bowl. Chop 3 hard boiled eggs and add to shrimp. Add to shrimp and egg mixture: Newman's Own Bandito Diavolo sauce, creole mustard, olive oil, cider vinegar and black olives. Stir ingredients and place in a glass or plastic container with a tight fitting lid. Refrigerate 24 hours and shake or stir several times.

For salad: serve over shredded lettuce. Sprinkle with thinly sliced green onions and garnish with a lemon or lime wedge. Yield: 8 salads.

For dip: omit lettuce and lemon. Serve with your favorite crackers.

This is a recipe I created for a Paul Newman's cooking contest. My inspiration was a combination of Shrimp Arnaud's and Mary Mahoney's Shrimp Italienne. I didn't win the contest but received accolades from Mom and Dad, Mary and Ron and other test-tasters.

Kathryn O'Keefe

Shrimp Boat Potato Salad

4 large red potatoes
2 pounds fresh shrimp, peeled and deveined
1 cup olive oil   2 bell peppers, chopped fine
1 cup Italian dressing   Salt and black pepper to taste
3 cloves garlic, sliced   Red pepper to taste
1 bunch green onions, minced

Boil potatoes, peel and slice in quarter-inch rounds. Place in a large bowl. Boil shrimp in seasoned water, drain and place over potato rounds. Add the remaining ingredients—garlic, onions and bell peppers seasoned with salt and pepper. Refrigerate and allow to sit over night for flavor to blend.

Gladys Eleuterius

Spinach Salad and Dressing

Salad Ingredients:
1 10-ounce bag of spinach, washed and torn in small pieces
6 slices bacon, cooked and crumbled in small pieces
6 green onions, finely chopped
1 orange, peeled and torn into slices

Dressing Ingredients:
1 egg
½ cup sugar
½ cup white vinegar
¾ teaspoon salt
1½ teaspoons bacon fat

Toss spinach, chopped bacon, green onions and orange slices. Beat egg, add sugar, vinegar, salt and bacon fat. Cook over low heat. Bring to a boil for one minute, cool and chill in fridge until ready to serve. Spoon over spinach.

Mercedes O'Keefe Huval

Spinach-Chicken Salad

6 boneless chicken breasts
1 cup soy sauce
1 cup sherry
1 tablespoon red pepper
1 tablespoon garlic powder
1 tablespoon ground ginger
1¾ cups olive oil
½ cup red wine vinegar
¼ cup cider vinegar
1 cup Parmesan cheese
1 bag fresh spinach leaves, washed and torn
1 head Boston bibb lettuce, washed and torn
1 head Romaine lettuce, washed and torn
1 pound turkey bacon (or regular) fried and drained
4 quartered hard boiled eggs
1 pound fresh mushrooms, sliced
1 box cherry tomatoes
1 can seedless black olives
1 can chinese noodles

Marinate chicken in soy sauce, sherry wine, red pepper, garlic powder and ginger. Brown chicken breasts in 1 cup olive oil until done. Add marinade to olive oil above and then add ¾ more cups olive oil, red wine vinegar, cider vinegar and Parmesan cheese. Heat mixture but do not boil for dressing.

Arrange salad on plates with chicken breast strips on top, garnished with bacon, eggs, mushrooms, tomatoes and olives. Spoon hot dressing over salad; sprinkle with Chinese noodles. Serves 12 generously.

This can be the main course at lunch.

Rose Annette O'Keefe

Buffet Salad Platter

(can be used to accompany beef tips recipe on p. 147)

Curly lettuce
Tomatoes, sliced
Cucumbers, sliced
Beets, sliced
Heart of palm
Asparagus spears
Artichoke hearts
Large green and black olives, pitted
Vinegarette salad dressing

Cover large platter with lettuce. Arrange other vegetables on lettuce. Drizzle with salad dressing. Amount of vegetables will depend on number of guests.

Rose Annette O'Keefe

Cole Slaw

1 large cabbage, shredded
3 carrots, grated
1 large onion, minced or grated
1 cup olive oil
4 lemons, juice of
Salt and pepper to taste

In large bowl shred cabbage with sharp chef's knife after cutting into quarters. Remove core of cabbage. Grate carrots and onion. Drizzle olive oil over mixture, then add lemon juice and seasoning. Toss well and serve. (If lemons are not available, white vinegar may be substituted.) Serves 10 to 12.

Rose Annette O'Keefe

Salad lovers all . . . (from left) Cecilia, Kathryn, Virginia and Susan O'Keefe (c. 1966 ?).

Refrigerator Salad

2 10-ounce packages of frozen peas
2 10-ounce packages of baby lima beans
4-6 carrots, diced
4 tablespoons green onions, finely minced
2 tablespoons lemon juice
⅔ cup mayonnaise
1 teaspoon salt
½ teaspoon pepper
2 teaspoons sugar
1 handful of finely minced dill pickle

Cook vegetables for 7 minutes, rinse in cold water. Beat lemon into mayonnaise and seasonings. Put vegetables in bowl, pour sauce over them, add dill pickles and cover tightly. Refrigerate for 3-4 hours.

Cecilia O'Keefe Neustrom

Mom's Salad Dressing

2 cups olive oil
½ cup cider vinegar
1 tablespoon Lea & Perrin Worcestershire sauce
2 lemons, juice of
2 cloves garlic, minced
2 teaspoons paprika
2 tablespoons salad herbs (see * page 39)
Salt, black pepper to taste

Mix above ingredients thoroughly.

For variety add ½ cup Parmesan cheese, and/or 1 cup crumbled Bleu cheese, and/or 2 tablespoons capers, and/or 1 tablespoon brown creole mustard.

Each time it is different, but always, always good!

Rose Annette O'Keefe

And those salad days . . .

Aug. 1, 1944
First Lt. J.J. O'Keefe

My darling,
This isn't going to be very long honey because I'm really dead tired tonight. This morning I got up at 6:30, took some exercises and a quick swim before breakfast and tonight played tennis and swam again so you can see that your ol' man is tired. All this exercise is making me feel good though and gives me a wonderful appetite. The food [here] is good but I would rather be eating food which you cooked than any other. Honey I really do miss those swell salads you used to make. I hope you know how much I liked them darling.
I was sort of hoping for a letter today but no mail came in so

Jeremiah Joseph O'Keefe (c. 1945) in U.S. Marine dress whites. As a fighter pilot in World War II, he shot down seven enemy aircraft in the Pacific theater.

I'll look for one tomorrow. Your letters always mean so much to me dearest that it just makes the whole day perfect.

Darling I'm so glad you feel the same as I do because you are everything in this world I have ever wanted and I thank God for being so good to me. I just know God made us for each other or we couldn't be so happy and contented. Honey, I too have lost interest in so many things and if I could only be with you everything would just be perfect. Things I used to take so much interest in before have just faded from my mind and you are now there with your pretty smile and visions of a little round-faced baby. Honestly honey this is the most wonderful thing that has ever happened to us.

Darling, I'm afraid I'm not very original so I'll have to use those same ol' words:"I love you." [The words] "I love you" may be much used darling but they are from the very bottom of my heart and I could just hug you to pieces, I love you so much.

Write soon my dearest wife.

Your loving husband,
Jerry

Creole Vinegarette Dressing

1 cup salad oil
½ cup red wine vinegar
3 large cloves garlic, crushed
1½ tablespoon Worcestershire sauce
1 teaspoon salad herbs (see * page 39)
2 tablespoons Creole mustard
½ cup Parmesan cheese
Juice and pulp of 2 large lemons
Salt
Pepper

Variation:
1 cup salad oil
½ cup red wine vinegar
1 egg coddled
3 large cloves garlic, crushed
½ can anchovies, finely chopped or 1 tablespoon of anchovy paste
1½ tablespoons Lea & Perrin Worcestershire sauce
½ teaspoon dry mustard
½ cup Parmesan cheese
4 ounces crumbled Bleu cheese
1 teaspoon salad herbs
Salt
Pepper

Chris Snyder
Variation by Rose Annette O'Keefe

Trilby's Salad Dressing

⅔ cup olive oil
⅓ cup garlic wine vinegar
1 tablespoon Lea and Perrins Worcestershire sauce
½ teaspoon salt
1 teaspoon black pepper
1 tablespoon paprika
2 teaspoons salad herbs*

This recipe was given to me in person by Trilby Steimer, who made Trilby's Restaurant famous. Her method of making garlic flavored wine vinegar is as follows:

Remove 1/5 from gallon of plain white vinegar. Add 1 bottle of any red wine such as burgundy, port, etc. Add several cloves of garlic that have been nicked or slashed on side. Voila! Wine Vinegar!

Rose Annette O'Keefe

* Salad herbs, if not found at your favorite food store, consist of one or more of the following: dried parsley, basil, chives, rosemary, tarragon, oregano, or marjoram. Use in the quantity given in recipe, or according to your taste.

Shrimp Italienne Salad Dressing

1 pound peeled shrimp
½ cup vegetable oil
½ cup distilled vinegar
2 hard-boiled eggs
1 small can tomato juice
1 teaspoon Italian seasonings

2 teaspoons Lea & Perrins
½ teaspoon garlic powder
½ cup celery
⅓ cup green onions
1 cup Greek olives

Rinse shrimp, add to salted boiling water and boil for 5 minutes. Cool and peel. Combine vegetable oil, vinegar, tomato juice, Italian seasoning, Lea & Perrins and garlic powder. Chop finely celery, green onions and eggs. Combine all ingredients. Salt and pepper to taste. Serve over mixed salads.

Mary Mahoney's Old French House
Variation by Maureen O'Keefe Ward

French Tartar Sauce

3 tablespoons mayonnaise
½ teaspoon dry mustard
½ teaspoon Gray Poupon or spicy mustard
½ teaspoon regular mustard
1 teaspoon sweet pickle relish
1 teaspoon minced onions
½ lemon
¼ teaspoon paprika
¼ teaspoon salt
¼ teaspoon pepper
½ teaspoon garlic powder
Several shakes of Tabasco (*optional*)

Put 3 heaping tablespoons of mayo into bowl. Add all mustards, relish and onions. Squeeze ½ lemon including pulp (no seeds) into bowl. Add all spices and stir until it is all one consistency and enjoy on fish, shrimp, etc.

Justin B. O'Keefe

Moma's Marinade

For smoked or fried turkey, roast, fish or most anything you want to roast or barbecue.
½ gallon Mazola oil
1 bottle plain yellow mustard
Salt, black and red pepper
1 large bottle Lea & Perrins Worcestershire sauce
1 whole bottle dried minced onion
1 whole bottle dried parsley
Juice of 2 or more lemons and cut up rind
1 bottle Tiger Sauce
1 bottle Pick-a-Pepper Sauce
White vinegar, wine vinegar, cider vinegar
Sherry wine, burgundy wine or whatever is handy
Kraft Bar-b-que sauce (or catsup)
Lots of fresh minced garlic

Combine, mix thoroughly, place on meat, chicken or fish and wait for a couple hours. Then cook.

Bon Appetit! This makes a large quantity and stores nicely in the refrigerator.

Rose Annette O'Keefe

Marinade for Steak or Roast

1 tablespoon ginger
1 tablespoon sugar
¼ cup salad oil

1 tablespoon dry mustard
½ cup soy sauce
3 cloves garlic, minced

Combine ingredients, stir well, place on meat and let stand at room temperature for 2 to 3 hours or more.

Maureen O'Keefe Ward

Barbecue Sauce

4 onions
6 cloves garlic
1 bell pepper (optional)
½ cup oil
1 stick butter
2 tablespoons Worcestershire sauce
2 tablespoons brown sugar (*optional*)
1 bottle Heinz chili sauce
Salt & pepper to taste

1 bunch celery
1 teaspoon mustard
2 lemons (halved)
3 tablespoons vinegar
2 bottles ketchup

Chop onions, celery, garlic, bell pepper and put in a large pot with the oil and butter. Add chili sauce, catsup, Worcestershire sauce, vinegar, lemons, mustard, brown sugar, salt and red pepper. Cover and cook, stirring occasionally, for several hours. Remove cover and let cool down for 30 minutes.

Kathryn O'Keefe

Mom's Barbeque Marinade

8-10 cloves garlic
½ cup yellow mustard
¾ cup soy sauce
2 tablespoon red pepper
1½ cups red wine vinegar
Juice & grated rinds of 4 lemons
Dash of Tabasco

2 cups cooking oil
1 cup Lea & Perrins
2 tablespoon salt
2 tablespoon paprika
1½ cups sherry
   (*or any wine*)

Crush garlic and add with cooking oil, mustard, Lea & Perrins. Add in soy sauce, salt, red pepper and paprika to taste. Mix thoroughly. Add sherry wine and vinegar, lemon juice and lemon rinds. Place on meat and let stand at room temperature for 2 to 3 hours or more.

Rose Annette O'Keefe

Seafood Sauce

1 gallon mayonnaise
16 ounces Lea & Perrins Worcestershire sauce
½ gallon and 2 cups horseradish
2 large green peppers, minced
¾ cup lemon juice
5 bunches celery, minced
5 bunches green onions, minced
1½ ounces dry hot mustard
2 tablespoons sweet basil
10 tablespoons Cavenders seasoning
2 cups sweet pickle relish
2 tablespoons salt
1 large bunch parsley, minced
4 tablespoons white pepper

Hand chop all vegetables; combine ingredients in order given; place in sterile containers and chill. Yield 2½ gallons. 1 tablespoon msg optional. 1 ounce per serving.

Lorelei Stroble

This sauce is wonderful served with lump crab meat on a bed of lettuce with crackers.

Stocks and Such

For a great flavored seafood, chicken, beef or pork stocks.
2 onions, quartered
2 large cloves garlic, quartered
2 stalks celery, coarsely chopped
2 or more pounds bones, shrimp shells, of your choice

Brown the vegetables and bones in a 350 degree oven. Cover with 2 quarts cold water. Bring to a boil, then simmer for 8 hours, skim if necessary. Add hot water as necessary to maintain 2 quarts liquid. Strain, cool to room temperature and then refrigerate. Discard any fat before using.

Jerry "Jody" O'Keefe, Jr.

Sauce Piquant

1 cup medium brown roux
> *(1/2 cup oil & 1/2 cup flour; for directions see pp. 54, 55)*

4 tablespoons oil
2 cups each: chopped onion, celery & bell pepper
4 bay leaves
1 large can peeled & chopped tomatoes
2 tablespoons minced garlic
2 cups tomato sauce
4 cups rich chicken stock
3 tablespoons Lea & Perrins Worcestershire sauce
Salt, black pepper, white pepper, cayenne pepper, garlic powder to taste
4 - 5 pounds of the meat or seafood of your choice, cooked and deboned. *(It can be more than one choice.)*

Sauté vegetables till tender. Combine vegetables and all remaining items except meat in a Dutch oven. Bring to a boil, reduce heat & simmer for 45 minutes or so. Adjust seasonings and add your meat or seafood. Simmer another 20 minutes & serve over rice.

Good for chicken, duck, alligator, shrimp, crawfish.

Jerry "Jody" O'Keefe, Jr.

New Orleans Shrimp Sauce

½ heart of celery, finely chopped
½ white onion, finely chopped
3 tablespoons chopped parsley
1 stalk green onion, chopped
6 tablespoons olive oil
2 tablespoons white vinegar
5 tablespoons horseradish
4 tablespoons Zatarain's creole mustard
3 tablespoons lemon juice
1 tablespoon paprika
½ teaspoon white pepper
½ teaspoon salt

Whip all ingredients together in a mixing bowl. Chill covered. Serve with boiled, peeled & deveined shrimp. Serve over crisp, shredded lettuce.

Jerry "Jody" O'Keefe, Jr.

Salsa Verde

1 bunch green onions, minced
½ bunch parsley, minced
½ cup watercress, minced
½ cup sweet bell pepper, minced
½ cup capers
2 cloves garlic, minced
1 tablespoon salad herbs or sweet basil
2 hard-boiled eggs, finely minced

½ cup wine vinegar
¾ cup olive oil
1 teaspoon oregano

Combine ingredients thoroughly. Serve with poached fish, pasta salad or green salad.

Rose Annette O'Keefe

Meunière Sauce

1 cup seafood stock - strained (from shrimp, fish, crab, etc.)
½ teaspoon minced garlic
3 sticks unsalted butter
2 tablespoons flour (all purpose)
¼ cup Lea & Perrin Worcestershire sauce
¼ teaspoon salt

In a saucepan bring garlic and stock to a boil, reduce heat and simmer 2 minutes. Set aside.

In another saucepan melt 4 tablespoons butter over high heat, add the flour and whisk till smooth - 10 seconds and remove from heat.

Put first saucepan on medium heat and gradually whisk in butter mixture till smooth. Reduce heat to very low and whisk in remaining butter about ¼ at a time. Gradually whisk in the Lea & Perrin Worcestershire sauce and then the salt. Continue whisking & cooking until sauce thickens (5 minutes).

Keep warm or reheat over a pot of hot water - not boiling. If it separates can be reconstituted by whisking in a little boiling water.

Jerry "Jody" O'Keefe, Jr.

Remoulade Sauce

½ cup tarragon vinegar
4 tablespoons Zatarain's Creole Mustard
1 teaspoon horseradish
2 hard boiled egg yolks, chopped fine
4 tablespoons mayonnaise
1 large rib celery, chopped fine
3 green onions & tops chopped fine
3 teaspoons paprika
Dash of thyme, garlic salt
Dash of Lea & Perrins Worcestershire sauce
½ cup olive oil
Salt and cayenne pepper

In a bowl whisk together all ingredients except olive oil. Whisk in olive oil at little a a time. Taste for salt & pepper. Chill well. If serving shrimp remoulade go ahead and add cooked shrimp before chilling.

Jerry "Jody" O'Keefe, Jr.

Hollandaise Sauce

For Seafoods, Steaks, Eggs Benedict, Asparagus, Broccoli, etc.

4 egg yolks
2 tablespoons lemon juice
½ cup melted unsalted butter
2 cups very hot water

In a bowl whisk egg yolks until smooth. Whisk in lemon juice until well blended. Gradually whisk in butter, blending well. If it thickens too much, whisk in a little very hot water. If it separates, whisk in a little boiling water.

Especially good with Eggs Sardou, see recipe on page 188.
Jerry "Jody" O'Keefe, Jr.

Aioli

1 cup vegetable oil, or olive oil
4 cloves garlic
¼ teaspoon lemon pepper
1 tablespoon wine vinegar

1 egg
½ teaspoon salt
1 teaspoon dry mustard

Place garlic in processor and chop. Remove garlic and set aside. Place remaining ingredients (except oil) in processor and blend for about 10 seconds. Add oil slowly to processor in a steady stream until mixture begins to thicken. Add garlic to processor and continue processing for 20 seconds. Yield: about 1 cup. Use steel blade for chopping, plastic blade for mayonnaise.

Bernice Simmons

Marchand de Vin Sauce

Great for broiled steak, or over sautéed veal!
2 tablespoons butter
1 cup sliced mushrooms
½ cup beef stock, hot
1 cup brown sauce (*see recipe on page 160, if necessary*)
½ cup dry red wine
1 teaspoon dry parsley flakes

Sauté mushroom in the butter till tender. Add the beef stock, and simmer for 5 minutes. Add the Brown Sauce and wine and simmer 25 minutes. Correct seasonings. Pour over or serve on the side with the steak.

Jerry "Jody" O'Keefe, Jr.

Almond Dill Sauce for Steak or Chops

¼ cup butter
1 cup almonds, browned in butter
¼ cup flour
1 cup plain yogurt
2 cups beef bouillon
2 tablespoons dill weed

Melt butter in saucepan, stir in flour. Cook on medium heat 2 minutes. Stir in bouillon and dill weed. Cook on medium until thickened. Stir in yogurt and almonds. Baste on meat while it is broiling.

Jerry "Jody" O'Keefe, Jr.

Avocado Sauce

1 ripe avocado, peeled and mashed
½ cup sour cream or sour half and half
1 tablespoon lemon juice
1 teaspoon grated onion
1 dash tabasco

Mix all ingredients, chill in refrigerator, and serve with corn chips as a dip.

Maureen O'Keefe Ward

Escargot Sauce

1 stick butter
1 cup Lea & Perrins Worcestershire
1 cup soy sauce
6 cloves garlic, minced
1 lemon, juice and grated rind
1 cup sherry

Mix thoroughly. Use to bake escargot, or use over fish fillets or broiled shrimp.

Mary Mahoney

Extra Good!!! Mary Mahoney, now deceased, was a very close personal friend of mine. Her restaurant, The Old French House, is internationally known for its fine food and friendly welcome—a tradition being carried on by Mary's son Bobby and her daughter, Eileen Pitalo. Make this place "a must" for dining out in Biloxi.

Rose Annette O'Keefe

SOUPS & SIDE DISHES

Jeremiah Joseph O'Keefe (c. 1993), a father to 13, a grandfather to 35 and great-grandfather to 1. A former state legislator and two-term mayor of Biloxi, he is shown here making a pot of his chicken-sausage gumbo. It's not just the recipe, he says, but being able to make it "with authority."

Red Beans and Rice

2 pounds dried red beans
2 large onions, minced
1 bell pepper, minced
4 stalks celery, minced
2 cups diced ham (*or 2 cups spicy sausage pieces*)
Salt, red pepper to taste

Wash beans, place in large pot, cover with water. Bring to boil, then add remaining ingredients. Simmer everything on medium low and add more water if necessary to make gravy. Add salt at very last after beans become tender, as sometimes it will cause beans to stay hard. Serve over steamed rice and it can't be beat.

I learned how to cook this dish while we lived in New Orleans.
Rose Annette O'Keefe

A note on how to make a roux . . .

Many of the recipes that follow in this section and others require the making of a "roux." A roux is a base used for thickening gumbos, sauces and soups. It is made by combining equal parts of flour and oil, or flour and butter, and then heating the mixture on a stove until the flour is cooked.

There are basically two types of roux. A white roux is taken off the stove as soon as the flour loses its taste, but before the mixture has a chance to turn color.

A brown roux is cooked a little longer, so that it has a light brown color—about the color of a cup of coffee with a lot of milk in it. The brown roux is used most often in this cookbook, and is most common in the cuisine of the Gulf Coast.

Florence's Gumbo

5 pounds fresh shrimp, peeled
6 large crabs, cleaned with back removed, then halved
1 cup flour
1 cup oil
6 quarts water
½ bell pepper, minced
1 onion, minced
3 stalks celery, minced
1 pound chopped okra
1 can tomatoes chopped
1 small can tomato paste
Kitchen Bouquet
Bay leaf
Lea & Perrins Worcestershire sauce
Louisiana hot sauce
Salt
Pepper

Make a roux of oil and flour, 1 cup of each. Cook on stove at medium heat until golden brown. Set aside. Chop finely and saute in oil ½ bell pepper, 3 stalks celery and onion. Add to seasonings, chopped okra, tomatoes, tomato paste. Season to taste with salt, pepper, Kitchen Bouquet, Worcestershire sauce, bay leaf, hot sauce and whatever else you can find. Add water to seasonings and then add roux. Cook for about 15 minutes, and add crabs. When the gumbo is starting to look like it might want to be ready, add the shrimp.

Florence Pettis

My mother, "Moma Ceci," brought Florence to help me out three days before Jim O'Keefe was born, and Florence stayed with us for 30 years. She was much more than a housekeeper or cook. She was someone to talk to, laugh with, and she knew all the secrets of each of us. Her spirit is still around our house as we recall the things she said and did in her particular Hawaiian/Portugese style. She is woven into the fabric of our life, our home.

Rose Annette O'Keefe

Chicken-Sausage Gumbo

1 capon or 2 hens, cut up
2 sticks butter or margarine
3 white onions, chopped
2 bell peppers, chopped
4 ribs celery, chopped
1 bunch green onions or shallots, chopped
4 cloves garlic, mashed
1 bunch parsley, chopped
2 tablespoons Kitchen Bouquet
Salt, pepper and cayenne to taste
1 teaspoon thyme
4 cups ham, diced
2 pounds hot smoked link sausage, cut into ½" slices
Cornstarch
3 tablespoons file
3 pints oysters (*optional*)
Large 10-quart pot
Rice

Cut up capon or hens. Melt butter or margarine and saute capon in it. Remove and saute in same pan the onions, bell peppers, celery, green onions, garlic and parsley. Cook down. Add boiling water to fill half the pot. Color with Kitchen Bouquet. Add the seasonings and replace chicken in pot.

At this point you can add the chopped ham and the browned sausage. Thicken with cornstarch which has been dissolved in cold water. Add file and simmer a couple of hours. Remove chicken and de-bone. Return chicken to the gumbo pot. Remove excess grease.

If you like oysters, add the oysters including the liquid and simmer another 10 minutes. Serve hot over bowls of fluffy rice. Serves 12-16.

Mayor Jerry O'Keefe

Turkey-Sausage Gumbo

1 whole smoked turkey
3 onions, diced
1 bell pepper, diced
4 stalks celery, diced
2 whole cloves garlic, crushed
1 bunch fresh parsley, minced
1 bunch green onions, minced
1 tablespoon Tony Chachere's seasoning
Optional: ham, tasso, shrimp

1 tablespoon Kitchen Bouquet
1 cup oil
1½ cups flour
½ teaspoon cayenne
1 teaspoon filé

To make stock:
Cut 1 onion into quarters (leave skin on). Cut 1 whole garlic clove in half (don't peel). Cut tops off celery and add parsley stems and any other vegetable trimmings. Brown in 350 degree oven for (30-45 minutes).

Put turkey in large pot. Cover with "cold" water. Add browned vegetables and bring to a boil. Reduce heat and simmer until meat is falling off bones. Strain, retaining stock and dice turkey meat. Refrigerate turkey meat until gumbo is almost done. Cut sausage into bite-size pieces and lightly brown in a frying pan. Put aside with turkey meat.

Add to stock with 2 chopped onions, diced bell pepper, 2 stalks celery and 1 crushed garlic clove, file, Tony Chacere's seasoning and cayenne pepper. Bring to a boil.

Meanwhile, make a roux (*see page 52 for directions*) with the flour and oil. Add parsley and green onions to stock. Spoon roux into stock mixture. Add Kitchen Bouquet for coloring. Add turkey meat and sausage.

Voila!! Gumbo!! Note: Always tastes better the next day.
                                        Kathryn O'Keefe

Jody's Crawfish Bisque

4 pounds crawfish tails (*if bought frozen, thaw 2 pounds only*)
1 large pan cornbread (9"x13")
4 large onions, chopped
4 large bell pepper, chopped
4 bunches green onions, chopped
1 bunch celery, chopped
1 bunch parsley, chopped
1 large can tomato paste
2 large cans skinned whole tomatoes, chopped, reserve liquid
2 cups medium brown roux (1 cup each oil and flour)
3 eggs
5 quarts water
Kitchen Bouquet
5 bay leaves
Lea & Perrins Worcestershire sauce
Salt & pepper to taste
200 cleaned crawfish heads

Make a roux by cooking and stirring 1 cup oil and 1 cup flour in a pan until medium brown. Set aside. Sauté onions, bell pepper, and celery until tender in a gumbo pot with 4 tablespoons oil, reserving parsley and green onion tops. Remove from heat.

Crawfish Heads:
Preheat oven to 250 degrees. Chop 2 pounds of the crawfish tails, (it's easier if they are still frozen). Crumble the cornbread into a large mixing bowl. Add ½ of the sautéed vegetables and ½ the parsley and green onion tops. Add the 2 lbs. chopped crawfish. Add the eggs. Mix well and season to taste with salt, pepper, Lea & Perrins and cayenne.

Stuff the heads, placing them stuffing side up on a cookie sheet. Bake them slowly, at 325 degrees, on top rack of oven until dried out and browned.

(*continued on next page*)

Mercedes and David Huval on their honeymoon in the Grand Caymans (c.1989).

Bisque (cont'd)

Bisque:
Reheat the remaining vegetables on medium high heat. Add the can of tomato paste. Stir in well & keep stirring, scraping bottom for about 1 minute. Add the chopped whole tomatoes and stir well. Stir in 5 quarts hot water. Add 5 bay leaves. Bring to a boil, reduce heat for a slow boil, and add your seasonings to taste.

Stir in your roux (you may not need it all), making sure it is well dissolved. Adjust bisque to desired color with Kitchen Bouquet. Add the baked crawfish heads, reduce heat to simmering. Allow to simmer at least 1 hour for flavors to marry.

Add the crawfish tails, parsley and remaining green onion tops. Adjust seasons to taste. Serve over a little rice in bowls with some heads with each serving. Serves 30, freezes well.

Jerry "Jody" O'Keefe, Jr.

Oyster & Andouille Bisque

1 stick butter
2 cups chopped andouille (or other good smoked sausage)
1 cup each: chopped onion, celery, bell pepper
3 tablespoons minced garlic
1 cup flour
2 cups shrimp or crab stock
2 cups oyster liquid
2 cups whipping cream
3 pints oysters (more or less)
1 pound jumbo shrimp, peeled and deveined
½ bunch chopped green onion
½ bunch chopped parsley
Louisiana hot sauce
Lea & Perrins Worcestershire sauce
Salt and pepper to taste

Melt butter in a pot. Sauté sausage, onion, celery, bell pepper and garlic over medium heat. Add flour and mix well, do not brown. Add crab stock, oyster liquid and cream while stirring slowly. Simmer slowly for 10 - 15 minutes—do not boil. Add seasonings to taste.

Reduce until just thicker than desired consistency. Add shrimp and oysters. Simmer another 4 - 5 minutes. Add parsley and green onion tops. Serve in a bowl with a small pat of butter on top.

Note: If the shrimp and oysters make it too thin for your taste you can thicken it with a standard cornstarch/water mixture.

Jerry "Jody" O'Keefe, Jr.

Corn & Shrimp Chowder

1 stick butter
1 cup chopped onions
½ cup chopped bell pepper
½ cup chopped celery
3 cloves minced garlic
3 tablespoons tomato paste
2 tablespoons flour
1 cup hot chicken stock
10 ounces cut corn (frozen or fresh cut off cob)
1 pound chopped shrimp or crawfish
2 cup heavy cream
2 cups milk
2 tablespoons parsley, chopped
2 tablespoons green onions, chopped
Salt and pepper to taste

Saute onion, bell pepper, celery, and garlic in butter. Add tomato paste and flour. Then add stock and corn. Add shrimp or crawfish, cream, milk, parsley, onions, and salt and pepper. Heat thoroughly, but do not boil.

Kathryn O'Keefe

For a variation, crab meat may be substituted for the shrimp for an equally delightful soup.

Moma's Turtle Soup

3-5 pounds chuck roast
   (cubed, leave fat on)
8-10 quarts water
Salt
Pepper
5 large onions, minced
6 stalks celery, minced
1 bunch carrots, grated
2 medium cans tomato paste
1 - 1½ cups flour
1 cup oil

¼ cup mace
6-8 bay leaves
Tabasco to taste
½ bottle Worcestershire
2 teaspoons Kitchen Bouqet
4-6 pounds turtle meat
2 sliced lemons
Sherry, to taste
4 hard-boiled eggs, minced
1 cup parsley, minced
1 cup green onions, minced

Bring chuck roast to a boil in water. Add salt and pepper. Grind onions, carrots and celery. Add vegetables and tomato paste. Make roux—oil and flour. Add to soup. Add seasonings—Worcestershire, Tabasco, pepper, bay leaves, mace and Kitchen Bouquet. Then cube turtle meat and add. Simmer and stir for 1-1½ hours. Add lemons for last 15 minutes. Serve with sherry, chopped egg and parsley or green onions.

This brings to mind the TV special on which I was invited to demonstrate my method of cooking turtle soup. The hostess came to my home with the camera crew and we set up the kitchen. Off to one side was an easel with a large cardboard on which my daughter Mary had nicely printed the recipe. I had all the ingredients ready to go and a brand new copper pot. Nancy, the hostess, warned me against beating the spoon as I stirred the pot, as all sound was magnified by a tiny microphone on my blouse. Nancy, tall, slender, blonde, had to remove her shoes and I had to wear high heels to put us in camera range of one another.

Everything was unrehearsed which added to the humor of the event. Nancy said, "Annette, why did you put the turtle meat in the last of the ingredients?" I responded, "That's a good question, Nancy! I'm wondering about that myself!" We both laughed. As

Moma's Turtle Soup (cont'd)

the program ended and Nancy made her concluding remarks, she and the camera man turned to me. Not knowing what to add, I gave a little Bugs Bunny wave and said, "Bye-bye, folks!" My spectators had a huge laugh and so did I.

Note: Since turtles are an endangered species, veal or beef in the same amount can be substituted to make mock turtle soup.

Rose Annette O'Keefe

New England Clam Chowder

1 pound bacon, minced
2 white onions, minced
2 cups diced raw potatoes
4 canned clams
Milk
2 egg yolks to thicken
(or 2 chopped hard-boiled eggs)

4 cups mild and light cream
3 tablespoons butter
½ bunch chopped parsley
1 bunch green onions
Salt & pepper to taste
Dash of cayenne pepper

Saute minced bacon and white onion. Add potatoes and simmer in very little water. Add clams, clam juice, milk and seasonings. Thicken to desired consistency with egg yolks and/or chopped hard cooked eggs. Add butter and cream. Do not boil—only simmer. Sprinkle with parsley and chopped green onions to garnish.

Rose Annette O'Keefe

27-Ingredient Chili

2 cans pinto beans
½ pound sliced mushrooms
½ cup butter
2 medium chopped onions
1 can Rotel tomatoes
2 cloves garlic, chopped
2 pounds ground beef
1 pound pork sausage
2 tablespoons flour
1-pound can baked beans
1 4-ounce can pimentos
1 30-ounce can tomatoes
¾ cup chopped celery
½ cup chopped sweet red pepper
½ cup chopped green pepper
1 9-ounce can chopped black olives
1 tablespoon chopped cilantro

Sour cream
Grated orange peel
¼ tablespoon chili powder
1 tablespoon oregano
Grated Cheddar cheese
2 tablespoons black pepper
1 tablespoon garlic salt
1 tablespoon salt
1 12-ounce bottle chili sauce
½ cup minced parsley

Melt butter in skillet. Saute onions and garlic. Add ground beef, sausage. Brown and drain. Sprinkle with flour, stir. Transfer to dutch oven or 8 quart big pot. Add pinto beans, baked beans and everything else except sour cream and grated cheese garnishes. Simmer 30 minutes. Skim off any fat that comes to top. Serves 20. Freezes well.

Note: Rotel tomatoes are a brand of spicy canned tomatoes with green peppers. Any brand Spanish style tomatoes can be substituted.

Myrtle Anne Saxon

Chili

1 pound ground beef
2 chopped onions
2 chopped bell peppers
2 cans stewed tomatoes

1 can corn niblets (optional)
1 can pinto beans or ranch-style
1 can kidney beans

Brown hamburger and onion. Add all other ingredients. Simmer at least 1-2 hours on medium heat. The longer it cooks, the better.

This freezes well. A good way to serve this is piping hot with side bowls of jalapeno peppers and grated Cheddar cheese to sprinkle on.
Janie B. O'Keefe

Chili

2 pounds ground beef
1 pound pork, cubed
1 small can tomato sauce
2 cups beef stock
3 cups water
3 bay leaves
2 cubes chicken bouillon
2 cubes beef bouillon
Salt and pepper to taste

1 teaspoon basil
6 tablespoons chili powder
1 teaspoon garlic powder
½ teaspoon oregano
2 teaspoons ground cumin
1 tablespoon black pepper
1 tablespoon onion powder
½ teaspoon cayenne

In a Dutch oven brown meats. Stir in all remaining ingredients, simmer two hours, stirring occasionally. Adjust salt and pepper to taste.

Jerry "Jody" O'Keefe, Jr.

Meat Ball Soup (Albondigas)

2 pounds ground beef
½ tablespoon garlic powder
½ tablespoon ground cumin
Oregano, 1 pinch
⅔ stick butter
1 cup diced tomatoes
½ cup diced green chilies
4 cloves garlic, chopped
2 medium onions, chopped
1-pound (small head) green cabbage, chopped
1 finely diced medium-sized zucchini
½ bunch parsley or cilantro, minced
3 quarts beef broth
Salt and pepper to taste

In a mixing bowl mix ground beef, garlic powder, ground cumin, oregano and a little parsley. Shape into 1-ounce meatballs. Put aside. In a large pot, saute butter, tomatoes, green chilies, garlic, onions, cabbage, zucchini and one half bunch parsley or cilantro.

Add beef broth. Just before broth comes to a boil add meatballs one at a time. Salt and pepper to taste. Simmer for 30 minutes. Top with parsley before serving. Serves 12-15.

Myrtle Anne Saxon

Maureen O'Keefe Ward and her son Will, in their home in Bethesda, Maryland.

Moma's Navy Bean Soup

2 pounds Great Northern Navy beans

6 quarts cold water	2 cans tomatoes, chopped
2 ham hocks	2 potatoes, diced
or 2 cups diced ham	2 cups parsley, chopped
2 large onions, diced	2 bunches green onions, minced
1 carrot, diced	2 cloves garlic, minced
4 stalks celery chopped	Salt, red pepper, black pepper

Put beans and ham bone in cold water, bring to a hard boil and cook until beans are tender. Reduce heat, add vegetables and simmer 2-3 hours. At the last, add parsley and green onions sprinkled on top.

Rose Annette O'Keefe

16 Bean Soup

Green Northern Beans
Large Lima Beans
White Baby Lima Beans
Green Baby Lima Beans
Navy Pea Beans
Black Beans
Pink Beans
Red Beans
Small Red Chili Beans

Lentils
Crowder Peas
Field Peas
Yellow Split Peas
Green Split Peas
Black-Eye Peas
Pigeon Peas
Pinto Beans

Mix all these beans together. Then use 4 cups for soup.

Soup:
Ham chunks or turkey tasso
1 large onion, chopped
2 stalks celery, chopped
½ bell pepper
3-4 garlic cloves, chopped
1 12-ounce can diced tomatoes and chilies
Salt and pepper or Tony Chachere's seasoning
1 bay leaf

Rinse beans. Place 4 cups of beans in a dutch oven pot and cover with water. Add seasoning meat (ham chunks or turkey tasso). Bring to a boil. Simmer for three hours. Add onion, celery, bell pepper, garlic, diced tomatoes and chilies, salt and pepper or "Tony's" and bay leaf. Simmer 1 more hour, stirring often. Add more water as necessary.

Kathryn O'Keefe

Voila!! (Tastes even better the next day). This is one of my favorite "Christmas Basket" items to gather; mix together and share with friends and neighbors. Find as many different types of dried beans and peas as possible. Mix all together and measure out in two cup portions into baggies. Include recipes and list of beans.

Rose Annette O'Keefe

Chicken Soup

6-8 quarts water
10-12 chicken parts
(*backs are fine*)
3 large onions, minced
6-8 stalks celery, minced
1 pound mushrooms, chopped
2-3 bunches green onions, minced
1 12-ounce package noodles or vermicelli
½ bunch parsley, minced

Soy sauce
Tabasco (or red pepper)
Salt
Black pepper
Corn starch

Boil chicken parts in water. When chicken is done, remove it from pot, debone and return to broth. Add onions, celery, mushrooms, green onions, noodles and parsley. Season to taste with salt, pepper, soy sauce and Tabasco. Thicken slightly with corn starch and water. Serves 20-25. Freezes well.

Rose Annette O'Keefe

Dallas Cowboy Soup

2 pounds dried white pea beans
6 quarts water
½ pound diced bacon
4 stalks celery, chopped
2 onions, chopped
2 carrots, chopped
1 pound diced ham
1 tablespoon chopped parsley

1 cup ketchup
3 cloves garlic
2 tablespoons sugar
2 tablespoons salt
2 teaspoons seasoning salt
1 teaspoon paprika
1 tablespoon Tabasco

In a large soup pot, cook ½ pound diced bacon for a few minutes. Add in celery, carrots, onions, green pepper and garlic and saute until vegetables become slightly wilted. Add in beans, water and remaining ingredients. Simmer for two to three hours, until beans are tender.

Maureen O'Keefe Ward

Jim and Janie O'Keefe.

Vegetable Soup

Soup bone or 2 pounds beef chunks
1 minced large onion
1 shallot (if available)
2 tablespoons butter
1-2 quarts water
2 cans tomatoes (chop and add liquid)
5 large carrots
5 large potatoes
3 large celery stalks
2 tablespoons parsley
1 heaping tablespoon sugar
1 bay leaf
Salt and pepper to taste

Brown soup bone or beef with onion and shallot in butter. Cut vegetables in large chunks. The amount of each can vary with preference and others could be added. Add to meat. Add seasonings. Cook at least 2 hours on low boil until soup thickens. A shallot give this recipe a special flavor.

Janie B. O'Keefe

Vegetable Soup

3 gallons water
4 pounds soup meat or chuck roast
2 cans tomatoes, chopped
2 large onions, minced
4 stalks celery, chopped
1 sweet pepper, diced
1 rutabaga, diced
¾ cup barley
4 carrots, chopped or sliced
½ pound green beans, popped in half
4 Irish potatoes
Salt and pepper to taste
1 tablespoon Lea & Perrins Worcestershire sauce
2 cups pasta

Boil meat in water. Add tomatoes, onions, celery and sweet pepper. Then add rutabaga and barley. Next add carrots. Then add green beans, potatoes, salt and pepper, and Lea & Perrins. Finally, add pasta.

Make this recipe in a large 4 gallon pot. It will amply feed 16 or more people a portion of soup and soup meat. The soup meat may be served separately if desired.

For quick and easy soup, use tomato paste and frozen vegetables, but the other is better.

Corita Johnson

Homemade Vegetable Soup

3 pounds chuck roast
Water
1 small can tomato sauce
1 regular can stewed tomatoes
1 chopped onion
2 stalks celery
1 package Manischewitz Vegetable Soup Mix (any variation)
1 large package frozen mixed vegetables
2 diced large potatoes
1 package dry beef stew seasonings
Tony Chachere's and red pepper

Boil roast in water with tomato sauce, stewed tomatoes, onion, celery and vegetable soup mix. Boil until meat is almost tender. Debone meat and chop up. Add frozen vegetables, potatoes and beef stew seasonings. Cook until potatoes are tender. Season with Tony's and red pepper.

Add water periodically to desired amount.

Minestrone Soup

1 quart water or vegetable stock
2 cans plum tomatoes, chopped with juice reserved
1 small can tomato sauce
1 cup celery, chopped fine
1 cup broccoli, chopped fine
1 medium onion, chopped fine
1 small carrot, shredded
1 cup string beans, chopped
1 cup fresh peas (*or 1 can*)
½ cup garbanzo beans
1 cup fresh spinach, chopped (*optional*)
1 4¼-ounce can sliced black olives
1 garlic clove, minced
2 tablespoons Italian herbs
Salt & pepper to taste
Pasta shells
Parmesan cheese, grated (*optional*)

Combine in a large pot water, tomatoes, tomato sauce and vegetables. Simmer for 30 to 45 minutes. Add black olives, garlic, herbs and spices. Continue to simmer 25 to 30 minutes.

Serve over pasta and have Parmesan cheese on table for individual preference. A fresh green salad and garlic bread are nice compliments.

I like to cook my pasta separately (according to directions), so it does not overcook and leftovers can be frozen.

Mary O'Keefe Sumrall

Home-Stewed Corn

40 ears fresh corn
5 medium onions, minced
3 large cans spanish style (Rotel) tomatoes, chopped
1 can tomatoes, chopped
2 sticks butter
Cavender's Greek seasoning
Tony Chachere's seasoning

Rinse corn, cut kernel tips from cobs, then scrape milk from remaining corn on cobs. Add onions, spanish style tomatoes, tomatoes, butter and, enough (very) hot water to cover mixture. Simmer on low until corn is tender. Add a plentiful amount of Greek seasoning and use Tony's in place of salt. To stretch mixture, you may add frozen niblets and frozen cream style corn. It does not alter the taste. Optional: for this amount of corn, 2 pounds of crawfish meat can be added to vary flavor.

Virginia O'Keefe Brown

Moma's Sauteed Squash

3 pounds yellow squash, cubed
2 large onions, chopped
½ cup olive oil
1 tablespoon black pepper
1 splash Lea & Perrins Worcestershire sauce

Brown onions quickly in large skillet coated with ½ cup olive oil. Put onions aside, add all of the squash and press down to also brown quickly in remaining olive oil. Add onions, Lea & Perrins and black pepper to squash. Toss, turn heat to low until ready to serve. Never add water to this and do not cover skillet. It should be tender crispy when finished.

From Moma Rose to Rose Annette O'Keefe

Baked Yellow Squash

3 pounds yellow squash
2 sticks margarine, melted
½ cup dried parsley
1 cup Parmesan cheese
3 tablespoons garlic powder
Salt, black pepper, red pepper, paprika

Grease large cookie sheet. Slice squash in half down the middle. Pour melted margarine over all and sprinkle lightly with other ingredients in order given. Bake at 350 degrees in oven until tender.

Rose Annette O'Keefe

Sauteed Squash

1 pound sliced zucchini
1 pound yellow crookneck squash
2 large onions (2 cups diced)
4 strips bacon, cut in small pieces
1 teaspoon ground cumin
1 teaspoon garlic powder
1 teaspoon crushed oregano
1 teaspoon basil
2 teaspoon salt
2 teaspoon freshly ground black pepper
3 cups diced fresh tomatoes

In a medium-sized saucepan, cook squash in a small amount of boiling water until tender; drain and return to saucepan. In a skillet, saute onion with bacon pieces. Add cumin, garlic powder, oregano, basil, salt, pepper to onion mixture; mix well. Add diced tomatoes; cook 10 minutes. Pour over cooked squash. Simmer over low heat 10 minutes. Makes 6-8 servings.

Potato Casserole

5 pounds steamed or boiled potatoes, peeled
2 sticks butter or margarine
16 ounces sour cream
1 small jar dried chives
2 tablespoons dried parsley
Tony Chachere's seasoning
2 cups evaporated milk (regular milk can be substituted)
Cheddar cheese, grated
1 tablespoon paprika

While potatoes are hot, add all other ingredients. Blend all ingredients together with mixer. Be generous with Tony's seasoning as this will enhance flavor. Top with grated cheese and sprinkle paprika on top. Bake at 325 degrees until cheese melts.

Virginia O'Keefe Brown

Brabant Potatoes

3 large white potatoes, unpeeled
Salt, black pepper, garlic and onion powder to taste

Bring a lightly salted pot of water to a rolling boil. Scrub potatoes well and cut into ¼ inch cubes. Boil until tender when pierced with a fork. Drain water and rinse under cold water until cool. Place potatoes in a bowl and season to taste.

Fry in a skillet in oil until golden brown on all sides. Do not try to fry more than one layer at a time as they will break up. Serve immediately or keep warm in a slow oven with the door cracked. (This will keep them crisp and warm until served).

Jerry "Jody" O'Keefe, Jr.

Quick and Easy Potatoes

1 gallon can new potatoes
1 cup melted margarine
1 cup dried parsley
Salt, red pepper, paprika

Open can, pour potatoes in colander and rinse thoroughly. Place in oblong backing dish, drizzle with margarine and parsley. Sprinkle with salt, red pepper and paprika. Bake at 350 degrees until nice and brown. Good accompaniment to grilled steak or fish.

Rose Annette O'Keefe

Sweet Potato Casserole

3 cups sweet potatoes
½ cup sugar
½ cup butter
2 eggs, beaten
1 teaspoon vanilla
½ cup milk

Boil and mash potatoes. Mix in sugar, melted butter, eggs, vanilla and milk. Put in 13 x 9 inch baking dish.

Topping:
⅓ cup melted butter
1 cup light brown or white sugar
½ cup flour
1 cup chopped nuts

Melt butter and mix in remaining ingredients. Sprinkle on top of potato mixture. Bake 25 minutes at 350 degrees. Serves 10-12.

Cecilia O'Keefe Neustrom

Spinach Casserole

2 packages frozen chopped spinach
1 8-ounce package cream cheese
1 stick butter
1 teaspoon red pepper
Tony Chachere's seasoning
Bread crumbs

Cook spinach according to directions. Soften cream cheese and butter in microwave. Drain any water off of spinach. Stir in cream cheese and butter with spinach. Add red pepper and Tony's. Sprinkle bread crumbs over top of casserole. Bake at 375 degrees until hot.

Virginia O'Keefe Brown

Spinach with Ginger and Peanuts

1 cup fresh spinach, finely chopped
1 cup raw peanuts
3 tablespoons vegetable oil
⅛ teaspoon fenugreek seeds
1-2 hot green chilies
¼ teaspoon salt
4 tablespoon grated ginger

Soak peanuts in water for 3-4 hours.

Heat oil in large skillet or wok, then toss in the fenugreek seeds after a few seconds. Throw in spinach, ginger, peanuts, chili and salt. Stir, cover and turn to low and simmer 5-10 minutes. Spinach should be lightly steamed, not totally soggy.

Sam Ward

Greek Spinach Pie

1 10-ounce package frozen spinach
1 15-ounce package ricotta cheese
1 egg
3 tablespoons Parmesan cheese
1 dash garlic powder
1 dash nutmeg
1 dash salt and pepper
Melted butter
4 filo leaves

Cook spinach according to directions and strain well—should yield 1½ cups. Mix in large bowl—spinach, ricotta cheese, egg, Parmesan cheese, garlic powder, nutmeg, salt and pepper. Divide the mixture into four (4) equal portions. Take one filo leaf and fold it in half. Put one portion on the bottom third of leaf and fold over, tuck, and fold again so no mixture can escape.

This should look similar to an egg roll when finished. Place on cookie sheet. Prepare the remaining portions the same way. Brush with melted butter and prick each pie with a toothpick. Cook in preheated oven at 375 degrees for 25-35 minutes or until golden brown.

Hazel Pitalo

Spicy Chick Peas

10-15 cloves garlic
2 15-ounce cans chickpeas
1 can tomato sauce
2-3 hot chilies
¼ teaspoon salt
3 teaspoons vegetable oil
1 teaspoon cumin
¼ teaspoon cayenne
½ lemon, juice of

Blend garlic and ⅛ cup of water in processor or blender to make paste. Heat oil in large skillet, then add cumin and garlic paste. Fry for 2 minutes until garlic begins to brown.

Add tomato sauce, stir. Add drained chickpeas, chilies, salt, cayenne and lemon juice. Stir, cover and simmer approximately 20 minutes.

Sam Ward

Spinach-Artichoke Casserole

1 large onion, chopped
3 sticks butter
1 tablespoons flour
2 12-ounce cans artichoke hearts, drained and chopped fine
1 jar marinated artichoke hearts, drained and chopped fine
4 packages frozen spinach, cook in microwave and press out liquid
2 cups sour cream
1 cup Parmesan cheese
1 dash of Tony Chachere's seasoning
5 eggs
1½ cups Italian bread crumbs

Saute onion in flour and 2 sticks butter. Mix with spinach and artichoke hearts. Sit in sour cream and ½ cup parmesan cheese. Season well with Chachere's. Beat eggs and fold in. Pour in baking dish. Top with mixture of 1 stick melted butter, ½ cup Parmesan cheese and Italian bread crumbs. Bake at 350 degrees for 30-40 minutes (until set).

Cover with foil if topping starts browning too fast.

Cecilia O'Keefe Neustrom

Stuffed Mushrooms

2 pounds fresh mushrooms
1 pound hot bulk sausage
1 stalk celery, finely minced
1-1½ cups Italian bread crumbs

1 stick butter
1 onion, minced
Salt and pepper
Parmesan cheese

Wash mushrooms. Cut off stems and chop about half of them finely and set aside. Brown sausage, drain and set aside. Saute chopped mushroom stems, onion, and celery in butter. Combine with sausage. Add salt, pepper and bread crumbs to the consistency of a stuffing.

Stuff mushrooms. Put in a buttered pan. Sprinkle with Parmesan cheese. Bake at 350 degrees for about 20 minutes or until brown.

Cecilia O'Keefe Neustrom

Stuffed Tomatoes

8 ripe tomatoes
2 sticks margarine
1 large onion, minced
6 green onions, chopped fine
½ sweet pepper, minced

1 cup parsley, minced
½ loaf stale French bread
1 tablespoon Lea & Perrins
Salt and pepper to taste
1 cup bread crumbs

Slice tops off tomatoes, scoop out pulp. Saute in margarine, onions, sweet pepper, parsley, pulp of tomato until done. Soak French bread in water, squeeze and shred bread into mixture. Add Worcestershire, salt and pepper. Stuff tomatoes, sprinkle with bread crumbs, dab with margarine. Place in baking pan with water to cover bottom of pan to prevent burning. Bake at 400 degrees for ½ hour, until tomatoes are tender.

Rose Annette O'Keefe

Cabbage Rolls

2 large heads cabbage
1 pound ground beef
2 pounds ground pork
1 large onion, chopped
½ bunch green onions, chopped
1 clove garlic, mashed
2 cans spanish style (Rotel) tomatoes
1 can plum tomatoes
1½ cup Uncle Ben's Rice
Garlic powder, to taste
Salt, to taste
Pepper, to taste
Worcestershire Sauce, to taste
Cayenne pepper, to taste
Oregano, to taste

Gently pull off large leaves from cabbage head and simmer in boiling, salted water about 5 minutes. Drain and lay out for filling. Also simmer remaining small pieces and drain.

Combine raw beef, pork, onions, garlic and seasonings to taste. (Test by cooking a small amount in microwave.) Mix in rice with beef mixture. Spray Pam in deep rectangular or square Pirex baking dish. Cover bottom of dish with small loose cabbage pieces.

Roll stuffing loosely in cabbage leaves to allow for rice expansion. Cover with crushed spanish style and plum tomatoes. Sprinkle with salt, pepper and oregano. Bake covered with foil in 350-degree oven for 45 minutes to 1 hour.

Hazel Pitalo

Hot Tamales

½ cup tomato sauce
2 tablespoons salt (or less)
8 tablespoons chili pepper (powder)
4 tablespoons Gebhart's Chili Quick
1 can spanish style (Rotel) tomatoes
1 can tomato juice
Water
3 - 3½ cups cornmeal
2 tablespoons and 1 teaspoon salt
1 tablespoon and 1 teaspoon red pepper
2 pounds ground beef
2 medium onions, grated
4 cloves garlic finely minced
1½ cups tomato sauce
60-70 tamales wrapped in shucks (coffee filters may be used)

Steam Mixture: Bring to a boil—½ cup tomato sauce, 2 tablespoons salt (or less), 2 tablespoons Chili Pepper (powder), 2 tablespoons Gebhart's Chili Quick, ½ can spanish style tomatoes, tomato juice and enough water to cover tamales and boil.

Cornmeal Mixture: Combine 2½ -3 cups cornmeal, 1 tablepoon salt, 1 tablespoon red pepper. Mix well.

Meat Mixture: ground beef, red pepper, onions, salt, garlic, 6 tablespoons chili powder, 2 tablespoons Gebhart's Chili Quick, ½ cup water, ½ cup cornmeal, 1½ cup tomato sauce, and ½ can Rotel tomatoes.

Drop shucks in boiling water - or use wet coffee filters. Drop one rounded tablespoon of meat mixture into cornmeal mixture and roll lightly, shaping roll about 2 inches long. Place on wet tamale paper and fold securely. Stack tamales in large saucepan on rack, pour steam mixture over, and cook for one hour 15 minutes.

Hazel Pitalo

Oriental Mushrooms

2 pounds cleaned, sliced mushrooms
⅓ cup minced onions
1 tablespoon teriyaki sauce
⅓ cup Lea & Perrins Worcestershire sauce
1 tablespoon parsley flakes
1 clove garlic, minced
2 dashes Tabasco
¼ teaspoon salt
¼ teaspoon pepper

Combine all ingredients. Start on high, then reduce to very low. Toss mushrooms constantly until they absorb other ingredients. Don't overcook.

Justice O'Keefe

This recipe is from a young grandaughter of mine. I am delighted to see her willing to experiment, and I predict a great future for her in the kitchen.

Rose Annette O'Keefe

Okra and Tomatoes

3 pounds okra, fresh or frozen
½ cup olive oil
3 large onions, minced
2 cans tomatoes, chopped
1 dash of Lea & Perrins Worcestershire sauce
Salt and pepper to taste

Wash okra, remove stems, cut in ½ inch slices. Pour olive oil in large pot, saute onions until transparent on medium heat. Add cut okra, stir well, add chopped tomatoes and seasonings. Cook uncovered until juice diminishes and okra is well done.

One of our favorite family dishes, typically Southern.

Rose Annette O'Keefe

Succotash

Use leftovers from Okra and Tomatoes recipe. Add yellow corn niblets and baby green lima beans. This recipe will take on a character of its own and is so good, possibly because the "leftovers" have become well blended by the next day. Frozen or canned corn and limas may be used.

Rose Annette O'Keefe

Susan O'Keefe Snyder lending a hand in the final preparations of a big Sunday dinner at the O'Keefe family home in Biloxi, Mississippi.

Green Beans

3 pounds small new potatoes
3 pounds fresh green beans, stems removed
2 medium onions, chopped
1 cup jalapenos, minced
2 tablespoons sweet pickle relish
2 cups diced ham
2 tablespoons Tony Chachere's seasoning
1 cup olive oil

Wash potatoes, put in large heavy pot with water to cover. Add ⅓ onions and ham to potatoes, then turn on high. Cook until potatoes can be pierced easily with a fork. Wash green beans well and add to potatoes. Pour remaining seasonings over all. Leave on high setting until boiling. Turn down to low and allow to simmer until well done and beans are tender. A dash of vinegar or lemon juice may be used when serving. Some prefer margarine.

Rose Annette O'Keefe

Marinated Carrots

2½ cups carrots, sliced ¼" thick
     (or 1-pound package cooked, but not too much)
½ onion, minced
½ can tomato soup
¼ cup salad oil
½ cup sugar
½ teaspoon Lea & Perrins Worcestershire sauce
½ (or 1 small) bell pepper, minced
⅜ cup vinegar
½ teaspoon prepared mustard
½ teaspoon salt and pepper

Marinate 12 hours. This will keep 2 weeks. Serves 8-10.

Also known as "copper pennies."

Bertha Tierney Carmichael

Marinated Vegetables

3 medium cucumbers, sliced ¼ inch thick
1 medium onion, sliced and separated into rings
3 medium tomatoes, cut into wedges
½ cup vinegar
1 cup water
2 teaspoons salt
¼ teaspoon coarsely ground black pepper
¼ cup oil
1 teaspoon chopped mint or basil

In a large serving bowl, combine cucumbers, onion, tomato wedges, vinegar, water, salt, pepper, oil and mint. Toss well to mix. Refrigerate at least 2 hours. Makes 6-8 servings.

Mary O'Keefe Sumrall

Baked Beans

1 pound large northern white beans
3 small onions, peeled
½ pound salt meat with streak of lean
Dark brown sugar
1 teaspoon salt

Parboil beans in enough water to cover, until they are half done. Put beans in 13 x 9" dish. Add salt and juice from beans to cover beans. Put onions, whole, on each side of beans. Cut salt meat in 1 ½ inch squares about ¼ inch thick, and parboil to remove some of the fat. Cover beans completely with salt meat. Add 1 large teaspoon of brown sugar on each slice of salt meat. Bake at 350 degrees until beans are tender and done. Note: If they dry out, add more of the bean juice.

Moma Ces and Aunt Caro

My mother raised me on baked navy beans—Boston style. My grandmother, Moma Rose, was a French Canadian and my mother, Moma Ces, was born in Salem, Massachusetts. Therefore I am not certain if the baked beans were Canadian or Massachusetts style.

Rose Annette O'Keefe

Beefy Baked Beans

1 pound ground beef
2 medium-sized onions, chopped
1 bell pepper, minced
1 pound mushrooms, sliced
3 tablespoons Lea & Perrins Worcestershire sauce
3 tablespoons ketchup
1 cube beef bouillon (dissolved in 2 cups water)
2 medium cans baked beans

Brown ground beef, onions, bell pepper and mushrooms. Drain grease off. Add ketchup, bouillon, Worcestershire sauce and beans. Bake in glass baking dish at 350 degrees until bubbly.

Susan Pitalo Jordan

Macaroni Marzelli

½ cup butter or margarine
2 pounds ground beef
3 medium onions, finely chopped
2 3-ounce cans chopped mushrooms
3 ½ teaspoons salt
¼ teaspoon garlic salt
⅛ teaspoon pepper
1 pound shell macaroni
3 cups grated Cheddar cheese
2 8-ounce cans tomato sauce
¼ cup Burgundy wine

Melt ¼ cup butter or margarine. Add beef, onions, mushrooms, 1½ teaspoon salt, garlic salt, and pepper. Cook until beef is brown, stirring occasionally.

Meanwhile, add 2 tablespoons salt to rapidly boiling water. Gradually add macaroni. Cook uncovered, stirring occasionally until tender. Drain in colander. Add ¼ cup butter or margarine and toss lightly. Turn into two greased 2-quart casserole dishes.

Add 2 cups cheese to meat mixture; stir until cheese is melted. Top with tomato sauce and wine. Sprinkle with remaining 1 cup cheese. Cover or wrap tightly for freezing. Freeze. Thaw casserole in refrigerator 24 hours before serving. Uncover and bake in slow oven (325 degrees) 1 hour and 40 minutes. Sprinkle with wine.

Annette Longeway O'Keefe

Spinach-Mushroom Pasta

1 pound fresh spinach, cleaned
4 large ripe tomatoes, seeded and cut into ¼ inch dice
6 scallions (3 inches of green left on), thinly sliced
2 tablespoons drained capers
6 tablespoons chopped fresh dill
¼ cup olive oil
½ pound shaped pasta (fusilli or bow tie)
1 pound white mushrooms: stems removed, cleaned and thinly sliced
2 hard-boiled eggs, grated
Salt and pepper to taste

Stack 8-10 spinach leaves, roll diagonally and cut in slivers; repeat until all are used. Place in a large bowl. Toss the slivered spinach leaves, tomatoes, scallions, capers, 4 tablespoons chopped dill, olive oil, salt and pepper in a large bowl. Set aside.

Cook the pasta in a large pot of boiling water. Drain and immediately toss with the spinach mixture. Divide pasta among 8 shallow bowls. Divide mushrooms evenly over each portion. Sprinkle with grated egg and remaining 2 tablespoons chopped dill. Serves 8.

Vegetable Noodles

1 cup sliced carrots
1 cup sliced zucchini
2 tablespoons butter
2 tablespoons olive oil
1 cup sliced fresh mushrooms
1 cup fresh chopped parsley
Salt and white pepper

1 large bag noodles
⅓ cup heavy cream
¼ cup chicken broth
Parmesan cheese, to taste

Slice carrots and zucchini to same size as noodles. Cook in boiling salted water sliced carrots (2 minutes) and sliced zucchini (1 minute). Strain vegetables retaining the salted water for noodles. Rinse vegetables in cold water to stop cooking and keep color.

Sauté mushrooms in butter and olive oil. Add parsley and salt and white pepper. Cook noodles and drain. Mix noodles and vegetables in large skillet with mushrooms. Add cream and chicken broth. Serve with Parmesan cheese.

Garlic Butter Vermicelli

12-ounce package vermicelli
2 sticks butter or margarine
1 cup olive oil
1 cup green onions, finely minced
1 cup parsley, finely minced
4 cloves fresh garlic, minced
1 cup Parmesan cheese (or Romano)
1 tablespoon Lea & Perrins Worcestershire sauce
½ teaspoon salt
½ teaspoon black pepper

Cook vermicelli in 4 quarts boiling water until just tender (al dente). Drain well in colander. Set aside. In saucepan, melt butter and add remaining ingredients, stirring over medium heat for several minutes. Put vermicelli in large bowl, add garlic butter sauce. Sprinkle cheese over; toss lightly and serve immediately.

This is a wonderful accompaniment to grilled or blackened fish. Delicious!!

Rose Annette O'Keefe

Dirty Rice

1 pound ground beef
1 pound ground pork
2 slices beef liver, diced
2 cups ham, diced
3 large onions, minced
2 sweet peppers, diced
3 stalks celery, chopped
2 bunches green onions, minced
½ cup Lea & Perrins Worcestershire sauce
3 teaspoons salt
3 teaspoons red cayenne pepper
3 teaspoons black pepper
1 whole bulb garlic, minced
9 cups long grain rice
3 quarts water

In large pot, brown beef and pork thoroughly. Add chopped vegetables and mix well. Then add Worcestershire sauce, salt and pepper seasoning and garlic at last. When well blended and simmered down, add rice and water, mix well. Cover with tight lid and cook over medium low heat. After 20-30 minutes, uncover, stir well, add more water if rice is not tender. When rice is done, cover and keep warm until time to serve. Serves 25-30.

We like this dish to be very spicy. Good for holidays, and to put in small casseroles for friends as a gift.

Rose Annette O'Keefe

Rice Pilaf

1 tablespoon butter
2 tablespoons olive oil
1-2 cloves garlic, minced
1 cup dry rice (or wheat/bulgur)
1½ cup liquid* (or more—usually not more than 2 cups)
1 small onion, chopped
1 tablespoon parsley
Salt and Pepper to taste

Melt butter and some olive oil. Add garlic and onion and saute. Add rice and cook for a few minutes (plain rice will turn translucent and then begin to turn cloudy colored). Add liquid. Cover and simmer about ½ hour (until liquid is absorbed) on low heat. Add extra seasonings to taste.

To be authentic, you can stir in a beaten egg after sauteing the grain but before adding the liquid. The egg, supposedly, coats the grain kernels and gives better separation. Cook with the egg a minute or two before adding the liquid. *May use chicken broth or part broth and water.

Maureen O'Keefe Ward

Oriental Rice

3 cups long grain rice
3 eggs, scrambled in margarine
1 cup diced ham
2 cups diced green onions
1 box frozen large green peas
1 cup soy sauce
1 cup olive oil (or canola)
1 tablespoon black pepper

Steam rice. When done, add scrambled eggs, diced ham, green onions and green peas. Add cooking oil, soy sauce and black pepper. Toss lightly and keep warm. Serve as an accompaniment to fried chicken or other meat dish.

Note: I usually triple the above recipe for our family.
Rose Annette O'Keefe

Jalapeno Hot Rice

1 medium-sized onion, chopped (½ cup)
1 medium-sized green pepper, chopped
2 jalapeno peppers, seeded and finely chopped
¼ cup butter, melted
1 4-ounce can mushroom stems and pieces, undrained
1 10-ounce can chicken broth, undiluted
1 cup uncooked rice

Saute onion, green pepper, and jalapeno peppers in butter in a medium sauce pan until tender. Add mushrooms, chicken broth and rice. Let mixture come to a boil, reduce heat and cover. Simmer 15-20 minutes or until rice is tender. Yield: 4 Servings.

SEAFOOD

*The Shannon-Toiresa shrimp boat, when she belonged to
Jerry "Jody" O'Keefe, Jr., the oldest son of the O'Keefe children. The
shrimp boat is named after his two oldest daugthers, Tess and Shannon. In
a nod to Irish tradition, he used the Gaelic spelling convention for
the name Teresa, née Toiresa.*

Boiled Shrimp or Crabs

¾ box salt
1 small bottle Zatarain's Liquid Crab Boil
6 lemons halved
½ cup cayenne
3 large onions, halved
3 bulbs garlic, halved
1½ dozen new potatoes, washed
1 dozen live crabs, preferably males
5 pounds fresh shrimp
1 dozen frozen corn on the cob halves
6 cups of ice

Experience is the only teacher that will give you perfectly cooked crabs and shrimp - it is always going to slightly vary your cooking times according to pot size, amount of water, heating source, and size and amount of seafood. Nevertheless the following is a good guideline to get you off on the right track .

If a crab is not alive when you add it to the pot, clean and save it for gumbo - as there is no amount of boiling time to make it turn out right.

Keep crabs refrigerated, this will make them retain their claws when cooked. Bring a suitably large pot with enough water to cover to a rapid boil.

While waiting for it to boil add salt, crab boil, lemons, cayenne, onion and garlic. Add potatoes.

If you are cooking shrimp, let the potatoes get about ¾ done before adding the shrimp. If you are cooking crabs let the potatoes get about ½ done before adding crabs.

Add the crabs and when the pot returns to a rolling boil, time 3 minutes. Add the shrimp and when the pot returns to a boil, time 1 minute.

(continued on next page)

Justin O'Keefe boiling crawfish, and making sure there's enough fire in the seasoning as well as on the burner.

Remove pot from the fire and add the corn. After 3 minutes stir in about 6 cups of ice, this will make the seafood sink to the bottom of the pot where they gradually cool and absorb seasonings.

Let soak at least 5 minutes, or up to 15. Boiling time for crawfish, 1½ minutes; for lobsters, 4 minutes .

Jerry "Jody" O'Keefe, Jr.

Cajun Boiled Lobster

3 gallons of water
6 ounces liquid crab boil
3 onions, quartered
3 lemons, halved
2 garlic bulbs

1 cup salt
¼ cup cayenne pepper
¼ cup black pepper
2 Maine Lobsters (1 to 1½ pounds)
1 stick margarine

Fill gumbo pot with water, crab boil, onions, lemons, garlic pods, salt and peppers. Let come to hard boil for several minutes to get water well seasoned. Add the lobsters, let come to hard boil, then time for seven minutes. Turn off heat and let lobster soak for 15 minutes. Make two butter cups with melted butter and ½ lemon squeezed in each cup. Serve and enjoy.

Justin O'Keefe

Stuffed Flounder

1 large flounder
2 sticks butter
1 stalk celery, minced
½ bunch green onions, minced
½ bunch parsley, minced

½ pound crabmeat
1 cup chopped mushrooms
French bread
2 tablespoons Worcestershire
Salt and pepper to taste

Saute celery, green onions and parsley in butter. Add crabmeat and chopped mushrooms. Wet french bread, squeeze excess water from it and shred into mixture. Season with salt, pepper and Worcestershire sauce.

Split flounder down the center of the top side. It is a good idea to remove the backbone, which is easily snipped out with scissors. Lift up both halves of fish flesh and stuff with dressing. Dot with butter and bake stuffed fish at 400 degrees until fish flakes off with a fork.

Cecilia O'Keefe Neustrom

Bacala

2 dried cod fish
10 pounds potatoes, peeled & quartered
3 large onions, minced
20 cloves garlic, minced
3 cups olive oil
1 bunch parsley, minced
2 lemons, quartered
Generous salt and pepper
Hot sauce (*optional*)

Soak cod overnight, place in very large pot and boil until fish is tender enough to fall from bones. Remove fish, discard skin and bones, break fish flesh into small, bite-size pieces.

Peel potatoes and place them in a large pot, then fill with enough water to cover them. Add fish and begin to boil. When all is tender, add onions, garlic, parsley, olive oil and cook until broth thickens slightly.

Serve in bowls with garnishings of minced garlic, parsley and plenty of lemon wedges. Louisiana hot sauce or Tabasco may be added for some pep.

This is a Yugoslav dish served in many variations on the Gulf Coast. The recipe above is how we like it, but it's good served very thick, almost like a salad, with the garnishings noted above, or served as a thin broth of potato and fish soup.

Rose Annette Saxon O'Keefe

Fillet of Trout Dunbar

1 6-ounce fillet of trout per person
Water to cover trout
1 pound plus 2 tablespoons butter
3 hard-boiled eggs, sieved
1 can anchovy fillets, mashed
1 bottle capers
1 tablespoon Worcestershire sauce
Juice of 2 lemons
1 tablespoon horseradish mustard
1 tablespoon onion juice
1 clove garlic, minced
Pimentos
Parsley
1 lemon, quartered

Wash fillets well, poach submerged in water and 2 tablespoons butter in 350-degree oven about 10 minutes or until done. Remove trout from water and allow to drain. Place on heated plate.

Melt 1 pound butter in saucepan. Add all ingredients to saucepan and simmer very slowly for 15 minutes. Pour sauce over fish. Decorate with parsley, pimentos and lemon quarters.

Redfish Courtbouillon

4 6-ounce redfish fillets
1 cup each, diced onion, celery, bell pepper
3 tablespoons oil
½ small can tomato paste
1 cup skinned, chopped tomatoes
1 cup medium brown roux
5 cloves garlic, chopped
1 cup sliced mushrooms
½ cup chicken stock
½ cup fine white wine
3 bay leaves
½ teaspoon each, thyme & basil
1 teaspoon salt
½ teaspoon Lea & Perrins Worcestershire sauce
1 teaspoon black pepper
¼ teaspoon cayenne pepper
½ cup each, chopped parsley & green onion
Steamed rice

Preheat oven to 325 degrees. Cut the 1 inch thinnest end of each fillet off for later use. Poach fillets in lightly salted water until firm, drain and set aside. Sauté the onion, celery and bell pepper in the oil. Add the tomato paste and chopped tomatoes, then sauté 2 minutes longer. Reduce heat to medium low, add the roux, garlic and mushrooms, stir well. Add 1 inch pieces of fish and stir in.

Gradually stir in stock and wine until well blended. Add remaining herbs, reserving parsley and green onions. Simmer uncovered, stirring occasionally for 45 minutes. Add parsley and green onion, cook 3 more minutes. Place fillets in a casserole dish, pour sauce over fish. Heat uncovered casserole dish for 10 minutes in hot oven (400 degrees) and serve over rice.

Jerry "Jody" O'Keefe, Jr.

Baked King Mackerel

1 5-8 pound king mackerel
2 large onions, minced
1 large bell pepper, minced
5 stalks celery, minced
2 bunches green onions, minced
6 cloves garlic, minced
1 cup olive oil
4 cups seasoned bread crumbs
Lots of black pepper
Salt to taste
Paprika
1 large lemon, sliced
1 bunch parsley, minced

Wash fish, remove head and tail if too large for roaster. Split down stomach and cut to backbone. Then remove backbone. Salt and pepper cavity. Saute minced vegetables in ½ cup olive oil. Mix in bread crumbs, blending well. Stuff dressing in cavity, garnish with lemon slices and paprika. Pour remaining olive oil over entire fish and place in roaster with 2 inches of water.

Bake at 350 degrees until fish flakes easily, approximately one hour. To serve, slice across and put fish and dressing on hot plate. Garnish with parsley and lemon. Serves 6-8.

This same method can be used to cook snapper, trout or any large fish.

Rose Annette O'Keefe

Poached Black Fish

2-3 pounds black (or red) fish
2 cups chopped onion
1 cup chopped sweet bell pepper
1 cup minced celery
1 cup minced parsley
6 cloves garlic, finely minced
1 cup minced green onions

1 tablespoon paprika
2 teaspoon black pepper
1 teaspoon salt
2 cups olive oil

Place cleaned fish in poacher (or on rack in roaster). Add water 1-2 inches deep. Use half of ingredients in cavity of fish and remaining ingredients spread on top of fish.

Pour olive oil over all, season with salt and pepper and sprinkle with paprika. Cover roaster and bake in hot oven at 400 degrees until fish flakes easily. Serve with lemon wedges and salsa verde. (See page 45 for salsa verde recipe).

This is a real gourmet specialty. As black fish are hard to get, red fish may be substituted.

Rose Annette O'Keefe

Trout Meunière

8 fresh trout fillets
Salt and red pepper to taste
1 egg
1 cup water
1 cup flour
1 stick margarine

Season trout with salt and pepper. Mix egg and water and dip fish. Then coat with flour. Melt margarine in heavy skillet, browning the fish slowly until golden brown. Remove to warm platter.

Meuniere Sauce:
1 stick butter, melted
1 clove garlic, crushed
1 tablespoon Lea & Perrins Worcestershire sauce
1 tablespoon lemon juice
1 teaspoon vinegar
1 tablespoon parsley, minced
1 tablespoon green onions, minced
½ teaspoon salt
½ teaspoon pepper

Combine above, blend well, put in same skillet fish were sauteed in, heat slowly, then pour over trout filets and serve right away. This goes well with brabant potatoes and tossed salad.

Arnaud's Restaurant in New Orleans is well known for this dish.
Rose Annette O'Keefe

Griddled Fish, Greek Style

8 trout filets, very fresh
1 cup olive oil
Salt and pepper
Paprika
1 tablespoon Worcestershire sauce
½ cup fresh parsley, minced
8 cloves garlic, minced
2 sticks margarine, melted

Heat griddle on high, sprinkle with salt to prevent fish sticking. When salt browns, brush away and pour light coat of olive oil on griddle. Put filets on immediately and do not move until edges are brown. Turn over with spatula, sprinkle with salt, pepper and paprika.

When fish flakes easily and is well done remove to warm platter. Combine margarine, garlic, parsley and Worcestershire, to make sauce. Spoon over fish filets and serve immediately.

Delicious with angel hair pasta or grits. Snapper, grouper, amberjack or trigger fish may be used in place of trout.

Rose Annette O'Keefe

Trout & Artichokes

6 6-ounce trout, triggerfish, or other pan fish
Salt, white pepper, lemon juice, all purpose flour
5 eggs, beaten
¾ cup clarified butter
6 cooked artichoke bottoms
½ bunch chopped green onions
3 cloves garlic, minced
½ cup your favorite dry white wine
½ cup lemon juice
8 ounces butter
Fresh chopped parsley

Season the fillets with lemon juice, salt and pepper. Dredge in flour and shake off excess. Dip into eggs, and sauté in hot clarified margarine until edges begin to brown. Turn fish over and cook until almost done (four minutes or so). Remove fish from heat until sauce is done.

In a saucepan add artichokes, green onion, garlic, white wine, lemon juice, salt and pepper. Bring to a boil and cut butter into three pieces and add all at once. Swirl and shake pan until butter is blended in well. Return skillet to heat. Pour over fish and garnish with parsley and paprika.

Jerry "Jody" O'Keefe, Jr.

Broiled Lobster Tails

12 lobster tails   12 cloves garlic
2 sticks butter   Paprika
3 lemons, quartered

Thaw lobster tails if frozen. Using poultry shears cut shell up center back, then tuck under lobster meat to raise. Place in broiling pan, put lump of butter on top, sprinkle with minced garlic and dash of paprika. Broil 12-15 minutes then serve immediately with drawn butter and lemon wedges.

Drawn Butter: Melt desired amount of butter over low heat. Allow to stand for solids to go to bottom. Skim clear liquid butter to use for lobster dip.

We used these to accompany a steak dinner for a special "surf and turf" effect. Simple—easy!!

Rose Annette O'Keefe

Giant Mushrooms w/Crabmeat au Gratin

12 - 14 very, very large fresh mushrooms, stemmed
1 pound fresh lump crabmeat
1 white onion finely chopped
¾ stick butter
3 tablespoons flour
2 pints half & half at room temperature
¾ cup white wine
2 tablespoons Lea & Perrins Worcestershire sauce
6 ounces Provolone cheese
8 ounces Brie cheese
Salt & white pepper to taste
6 - 7 slices lightly toasted bread, crusts removed

Preheat oven to 325 degrees. Sauté the onion in the butter till tender. Stir in flour and cook 2 minutes while stirring.

When adding the following liquids, allow the mixture to thicken and reheat before adding more. You want to finish up with a mixture with the thickness of a medium thick gravy. Gradually add the half & half while stirring. Keep heat high enough to keep mixture well heated so it will continue to thicken but not boil.

Gradually stir in wine. Stir in Lea & Perrins, salt, pepper. Stir in grated Provolone cheese, stir till melted. Remove from heat and gently add the lump crabmeat. Don't break up the lumps.

Place the cleaned mushrooms upside-down on a greased baking sheet and gently spoon the crabmeat mixture on the mushrooms.

Clean off any residue on the outside of the Brie cheese. Melt the Brie in a sauce pan. Pour a little Brie over each of the mushrooms. Bake the mushrooms for 20 minutes.

(continued on next page)

Joe O'Keefe (c. 1984) after a day of deep-sea fishing in Destin, Florida with Mom. The day's catch was a 70-pound yellowfin tuna.

Stuffed Mushrooms (cont'd)

Turn oven to broil. Broil until cheese is lightly toasted (watch closely). Serve immediately placing 2 mushrooms on each slice of toast.

My version of Trilby's recipe.

Jerry "Jody" O'Keefe, Jr.

Trilby Steimer was a lady known for her fine restaurant (by the same name) in Ocean Springs, Mississippi. For many years her cuisine was rated tops on the Gulf Coast, and after her death the tradition was continued. Jack and Jane Gottsche bought the business, and it is now know as Germaine's, and enjoying a fine reputation of its own.

Rose Annette O'Keefe

Corita's Stuffed Crabs

5 pounds fresh crab claw meat
1-pound container bread crumbs
5 loaves stale french bread
5 large eggs
3 sticks margarine
5 large onions, minced
Lea & Perrin Worcestershire sauce
3 bunches green onions, minced
5 medium sweet green peppers, diced
8 stalks celery, finely minced
2 tablespoons red pepper
1 tablespoon thyme
1 bunch parsley, minced
Salt and pepper to taste

Combine all minced seasonings, saute in 1 stick margarine until tender, not brown. Soak stale bread in water, then squeeze until just moist. Sauté in 2 sticks margarine until mixture dries and cooks down. Put aside to cool.

Add whipped eggs to bread mixture and stir well. Add to sauteed vegetables. Add crab meat and then all spices and Worcestershire sauce. Mix thoroughly. Cook a few minutes longer for eggs to pull mixture together. Then shape into patties or stuff shells. Sprinkle bread crumbs on shells or both sides of patties. Put on a large tray to freeze. When frozen put in zip-lock bags for storage in freezer unless they are used immediately. To serve, dot with butter and bake in medium oven (350 degrees) until brown or saute in margarine or oil in skillet until brown. Yield: 5 dozen or so crab patties.

Corita Johnson

Stuffed Crabs

2 pounds fresh crabmeat *(1 pound claw, 1 pound white)*
2 loaves stale french bread
Milk
3 eggs, lightly beaten
2 large white onions, chopped
2 large red onions, chopped
3 bell pepper, chopped
4 stalks celery, chopped
2 bunches green onions, chopped
1 bunch parsley, chopped
1 teaspoon cayenne pepper
1 teaspoon black pepper
1 tablespoon salt
½ teaspoon garlic salt
3 tablespoons Lea & Perrins Worcestershire sauce
Shells for stuffing the crabs

Reserve parsley and green onion tops and sauté remaining vegetables until tender. Remove vegetables to large mixing bowl, add parsley and green onion tops. Add seasonings and mix thoroughly. In another mixing bowl break up the french bread and soak it in milk, squeeze out all you can and finely shred the bread into the vegetables. Pick through the crabmeat and remove any crab shell found. Gently fold the crabmeat, eggs and green onion tops into the vegetables. Mix gently but thoroughly. Adjust salt & pepper to taste. Stuff the crab shells.

Fry in oil, mixture side down until well browned, then bake in a 350-degree oven for about 10 - 12 minutes.

This same stuffing is great inside baked Cornish hens or boneless chicken breasts and for a real treat, try it between two flounder filets baked in the oven with lemon and butter!! (Known as Captain Jody's Flounder Sandwich)

Jerry "Jody" O'Keefe, Jr.

Mert's Easy, Easy Etoufee

1 pound crawfish tails or 1 pound shrimp, peeled
½ stick butter or margarine
½ chopped onion
½ chopped bell pepper
1 can spanish style (Rotel) tomatoes
1 can cream of mushroom soup
Cooked rice

Saute onion and bell pepper in butter until soft. Add Rotel tomatoes, cook on medium heat for 20 minutes. Add cream of mushroom soup. Mix well and let cook down for 15 minutes. Add crawfish tails or shrimp. Cook for 20 minutes or until tails or shrimp are done. If too thick add a bit of water, mix well. Serve over rice.

Mercedes O'Keefe Huval

Jerry "Jody" O'Keefe, Jr., the oldest son of the 13 O'Keefe children.
His culinary knowledge is rich and storied: ranging from his political years,
rubbing elbows with country lawmakers in the state legislature, to his time as a
shrimp boat captain in the Gulf of Mexico.

Jody's Crawfish Etoufee

¾ stick butter
4 large onions, chopped
2 large bell peppers, chopped
4 ribs celery, chopped
½ head garlic, minced
1 bunch green onions, chopped
2 tablespoons tomato paste
3 pounds crawfish tails

½ bunch parsley, minced
Cornstarch
Worcestershire sauce
Salt
Black pepper
Red pepper
4-6 cups chicken boullion

Saute onions, bell peppers, celery, garlic and white part of green onions in butter. Add tomato paste, brown slightly. Add crawfish tails and bouillion. Season with red pepper, black pepper, salt and worcestershire sauce. Simmer ½ hour. Correct seasoning and thicken lightly with cornstarch. Add green onion tops and parsley. Serve over rice.

Jerry "Jody" O'Keefe, Jr.

Crawfish or Shrimp Etoufee

¼ cup oil
⅓ cup flour
1 cup each; chopped onion, celery and bell pepper
2 cloves garlic, minced
1 pound crawfish tails or peeled deveined shrimp
2 cups chicken bouillon (a rich chicken stock is better)
2 bay leaves
¼ cup chopped parsley
½ bunch chopped green onions, reserve tops
2 tablespoons Lea & Perrins Worcestershire sauce
Salt, pepper and Louisiana hot sauce to taste

Pour oil in black iron skillet, stir in flour. Cook on medium-low until roux is brown, stir very often. Add onions (except green onion tops), celery and bell pepper and garlic. Cook until tender.

Add seafood, stock, bay leaf, a little salt and pepper. Simmer 15 -20 minutes and adjust seasoning. Serve over hot rice with garlic bread and green salad.

Tips:
1) The store bought roux works just as well and saves time.
2) You can skip the roux altogether - just thicken with cornstarch/water mixture and use Kitchen Bouquet for color.
3) Some like to add a tablespoon or two of tomato paste for a slightly different flavor and color.
4) Using butter instead of oil for a roux gives a very different flavor, but still very good - give it a try sometime!
Jerry "Jody" O'Keefe, Jr.

Kathryn's Crawfish Etoufee

2 pounds peeled crawfish tails
1 stick margarine or ¼ cup olive oil
1 cup chopped onion
½ cup chopped bell pepper
½ cup chopped celery
1½ cups cold water
2 teaspoons cornstarch
¼ cup green onion tops and parsley

Seasoning mixture:
½ teaspoon cayenne pepper
2 teaspoons salt
1 teaspoon white pepper
1 teaspoon black pepper
½ teaspoon basil
½ teaspoon thyme

Saute onion, bell pepper and celery in margarine or oil until tender. Add crawfish tails, 1 cup water and seasoning mixture. Bring to a boil, then reduce heat and simmer for about 30 minutes. Dissolve cornstarch into ½ cup water. Add to mixture. Add green onion tops and parsley. Cook another ten minutes. Serve over cooked rice with hot french bread on the side. Serves 4.

Kathryn O'Keefe

Rose Annette and Jerry O'Keefe coming home with a catch after a trip with Capt. William Frank Davis. Says Rose Annette, "We've never had a bad day with William Frank or his son, Capt. Tony Davis, fishing out of Destin, Florida. They both are tops!! You can find them aboard the Anastasia I or Anastasia II."

Curried Shrimp

1 pound shrimp, shelled and deveined
1 medium onion, minced
½ pound mushrooms, sliced
2 teaspoons sherry
1 tablespoon curry powder
2 tablespoons cornstarch
2 tablespoons peanut oil
2 slices ginger root, ⅛" thick, minced fine

1 cup frozen peas
2 teaspoons soy sauce
2 cloves garlic, minced
1½ cups chicken broth

Using wok or skillet, heat ginger and garlic in oil until golden brown. Add shrimp, stir until pink, put aside. Add more oil and sauté onions, mushrooms and peas for two minutes with soy and sherry. Add ½ cup chicken broth, curry powder, cornstarch and then the rest of chicken broth. Simmer until it thickens. Return shrimp to mixture, stir well and serve over steamed rice.

Lucy Mavar

Delicious and light!

Jody's Jambalaya

4 pounds meats
(your pleasure, chicken, shrimp, oysters, pork, or combo)
1 pound smoked sausage, sliced in ½ inch pieces
Cooking oil
5 large onions, chopped
4 stalks celery, chopped
4 large bell pepper, chopped
½ small can tomato paste (optional)
Rice
Water
Lea & Perrins Worcestershire sauce
Salt, black pepper, cayenne
1 or 2 pounds fresh picked crabmeat
1 bunch green onions, chopped, tops reserved
½ bunch parsley, minced

To start with, cook your meats in enough lightly salted and peppered stock to cover in the large pot you will wind up in. Fresh or even frozen chicken, pork or shrimp/seafood stock rather than the salted water is so much the better. If you do not have any stock around add a few chicken bouillon cubes.

Bring the pot of water and meats to a boil and lower heat to slow boil. If using seafood only, remove from heat and remove seafood after 4 minutes. If using meat only, or a meat /seafood combo, parboil meat until well done.

While pot is cooking, fry the sausage in a skillet with a small amount of cooking oil until well done on both sides - stir and fiddle with frequently until done. If you are using lean, boneless pork it should be fried also rather than boiled. Remove sausage pieces as they cook and set aside.

(Store this out of sight, or it will be gone before you need it again. Only the cook should test the sausage at this stage).

continued on next page

Jambalaya (cont'd)

Add all vegetables except the green onion tops and parsley and sauté until done. If you are using the tomato paste, add it now. Deglaze the skillet with a little of the stock from your pot and set aside. By now your meats should be ready to cool and debone. Remove from the pot, saving all of the stock. Cool in a colander under cold running water and debone.

Before beginning your rice, add seasonings to taste to the stock, then add a little extra to make up for the volume of rice and meats, along with the deglazed juices.

Now, using your recipe for rice on your particular brand of rice, measure the rice to match the amount of water left in your pot for correct proportions. If you went overboard on the water you may have to remove some of the stock. Use your own judgment, but leave room to add your meats when the rice and water have doubled in volume.

Cook your rice according to your directions until done. If using crabmeat, fold in lightly, last. Add your sausage, vegetables and meats, green onions, parsley and stir in well. Serve with hot garlic french bread and a green salad.

This recipe is the result of years of trial and error, borrowing ideas and finally coming up with a great meat, seafood, meat/seafood combination jambalaya. This recipe is my own, but the product of many other cooks.

I prefer, as do most cooks from Acadiana, omitting the tomato paste, but some insist on it for color and flavor, neither of which amount to much. If I haven't talked you out of it, stir it on in now.
                                        Jerry "Jody" O'Keefe, Jr.

Shrimp - Manales Style

3 pounds jumbo shrimp in the shell, washed well
(heads left on produces a better flavored dish)
1½ pounds butter
1 bunch chopped green onion
5 cloves minced garlic
½ cup olive oil
½ cup good white wine
4 tablespoons Lea & Perrins Worcestershire sauce
Juice of 4 lemons
3 tablespoons salt
½ large can of black pepper
(That's right 1/2 large can! Trust me on this!)

Preheat oven to 350 degrees. In a deep baking pan place the shrimp. Melt the butter and pour over the shrimp. Add remaining ingredients except green onion. Stir sauce in well and toss shrimp around to coat well. Bake 45 minutes, turn the shrimp in the sauce every once in a while to insure even cooking, bring those from the bottom up to the top.

While it's baking prepare your garlic french bread. Put it in during the last 5 minutes. When you put the bread in, stir in the green onions with the shrimp.

Serve the shrimp in bowls with some of the sauce and a bowl on the side for shells. Dip your french bread in that sauce for a taste delight. Purists and fanciers of this cooking technique eat the shrimp, shell and all! I do too!

Jerry "Jody" O'Keefe, Jr.

Shrimp New Orleans Style

3 pounds shrimp, peeled and deveined
Icy cold lettuce

Sauce:
1 cup olive oil
1 cup creole mustard (brown kind)
½ cup horseradish
2 tablespoons paprika
½ cup green onions, finely minced
½ cup celery, finely minced
½ cup lemon juice
½ cup cider vinegar
Salt, red pepper, black pepper to taste
1 teaspoon hot pepper sauce
1 clove garlic, crushed

Simmer shrimp in small amount of water. Shred lettuce and place on salad plates to make a bed for shrimp. Put 8-10 shrimp on each plate. Spoon sauce over each serving, or shrimp may be marinated in sauce overnight in refrigerator.

This sauce will clear out your sinuses and make you dance a jig. Use French crusty bread to "sop" sauce after shrimp are gone. You'll want more!!

Rose Annette O'Keefe

Fried Shrimp Mercedes

3 pounds raw shrimp, peeled and deveined
1½ cups flour
2 cups milk
6 eggs, beaten
Black pepper
2 cups cooking oil

Make batter with flour, milk, eggs and pepper. Marinate shrimp three hours, then dip them back in plain flour. Fry shrimp a few at a time until golden brown, changing oil if necessary. Remove from oil, drain on brown paper bag, salt and pepper lightly. Serve at once.

Mercedes Williams Hall

This is positively the best fried shrimp we have ever tasted. You'll "come back for more." Mercedes Hall and her husband Leon owned and operated De Jean Packing Company many years. The company began with her father Elmer Williams and his brothers. Their products could be found the world over and we found De Jean shrimp on the shelf in Germany. They, like other seafood companies, have succumbed to the gambling casinos, but it was seafood that first made Biloxi, Mississippi famous. This recipe will make you famous, "win friends and influence people," I guarantee!!

Rose Annette O'Keefe

How to Make a Po'Boy

A Po'Boy is a special kind of sandwich found mostly in the deep South—I would say primarily between New Orleans and Mobile. It requires a French bread, known as Po'Boy bread, which comes in a long and slender loaf that is not as thick as the traditional French loaf. It has a soft center and a nice crusty outside which becomes very crispy when it is heated. One always prepares the loaf while it is at room temperature and after the filling and dressing is added, it is then put on a hot griddle, or in a heavy skillet, and pressed down while it heats.

There are many types of Po'Boys and some favorites here in Biloxi are roast beef, ham, with or without cheese, fried shrimp, fried oyster, crabmeat, crabmeat and cheese (known as the Vancleave special), meatball, soft shell crab, and almost anything your imagination can contrive. You are usually asked if you want yours "fully dressed" which means with mayonnaise, lettuce and tomato or with "gravy only", as in the case of roast beef. P.S. The crab meat is a crab dressing just like you would use to make stuffed crabs or patties. I promise you, after you try one, you will want another very soon.

Rose Annette O'Keefe

Shrimp Breading

1 quart buttermilk	Shrimp
½ teaspoon salt	Waxed paper
1 teaspoon paprika	Cardboard beer flat
1 tablespoon garlic powder	
1 ½ tablespoons red pepper	
Cracker meal	

Mix well and soak cleaned and deveined shrimp in buttermilk and seasonings for about 15 minutes. Roll in cracker meal and lay on paper in flat in layers. Tape paper on top of flat and freeze until ready to use. Fry and enjoy.

Shrimp Croutons

2 drained cans of shrimp
2 cans cream of mushroom soup
1 package of cream cheese
½ bunch parsley, minced
1 cup chopped onions
Salt, pepper to taste
Fresh bread
Cheddar cheese, grated
Paprika

Heat shrimp, mushroom soup, cream cheese, parsley, onions and seasoning. Cut crusts off fresh bread, put a slice in each muffin pan hole. Fill with sauce, top with cheddar cheese and paprika. Bake at 375 degrees until tops of bread are brown.

Maureen O'Keefe Ward

Shrimp Victoria

1 pound raw shrimp, peeled
1 small onion, finely chopped
¼ cup butter or margarine
1 6-ounce can mushrooms
1 tablespoon flour
1 dash cayenne pepper
¼ teaspoon salt
1 cup sour cream
1½ cups cooked rice
Parsley (*optional*)
White wine (*optional*)

Saute shrimp and onion in butter or margarine for 10 minutes or until shrimp are tender. Add mushrooms and cook for 5 minutes more. Sprinkle in flour, salt, and pepper. Stir in sour cream and cook gently for 10 minutes, not allowing mixture to boil. White wine added toward the end of cooking adds a special flavor. Serve over rice. Add parsley to rice for color. Makes 4-6 servings.

Janie B. O'Keefe

Grilled Shrimp Brochette

2 pounds fresh jumbo shrimp, headless
2 pounds fresh shishkabob vegetables:
    Cherry tomatoes
    Bell pepper
    Onion
    Mushrooms

Marinade:
2 cups soy sauce
¾ cup white wine or sherry
3 large lemons, taking juice and rinds of 1 lemon
1 cup olive oil
5 large cloves garlic, crushed
1 teaspoon oregano leaves
1 tablespoon basil leaves
3 tablespoons paprika
½ teaspoon cayenne pepper
1 teaspoon onion powder
1 teaspoon black pepper

Peel, devein and butterfly shrimp. Wash and cut vegetables.
Marinate shrimp and vegetables in refrigerator for one hour.

Make up shishkabobs. Grill and smoke over hot coals and
hickory or mesquite wood chips (cover grill) approximately
5 minutes on each side or until shrimp are lightly toasted.

Captain Jody a.k.a. Jerry "Jody" O'Keefe, Jr.

Stir Fried Shrimp with Lobster Sauce

1 pound shrimp, peeled & deveined
¼ cup peanut oil
1 tablespoon sherry
2 teaspoons fermented black beans, chopped (optional)
1 teaspoon minced garlic
¼ pound ground lean pork (can substitute pork sausage)
1 tablespoon soy sauce
¼ teaspoon sugar
¼ teaspoon freshly ground black pepper
2 green onions, including tops, chopped
1 cup chicken stock, fresh or canned
2 tablespoons cornstarch dissolved in 3 tablespoons cold chicken stock
2 eggs, lightly beaten

Heat wok or skillet over high heat for 30 seconds. Add 4 tablespoons oil and heat for 30 seconds, reduce heat if oil begins to smoke. Add shrimp and stir fry about 1 minute or until pink. Stir in wine and remove mixture to a plate.

Add remaining oil to pan, add black beans and garlic, stir a few seconds. Add the pork and stir fry 2-3 minutes till no longer pink. Stir in soy sauce, sugar, pepper, onion and reserved shrimp.

Add chicken stock, cover and bring to a boil. Combine cornstarch mixture and add to pan. When sauce has thickened and become clear (about 30 seconds), pour in eggs in a slow stream, meanwhile with a large spoon, lift contents of the pan gently from the sides so the eggs merge with all of the ingredients. Transfer to a heated platter and serve at once. Best served over rice.

Jerry "Jody" O'Keefe, Jr.

Stir Fried Shrimp

2 tablespoons peanut or other vegetable oil
1 tablespoon fresh ground ginger
1 teaspoon minced garlic
4 green onions, including tops, cut into ¼ inch pieces
¼ teaspoon cayenne
1 pound peeled and deveined large shrimp
1 tablespoon sherry
2 tablespoons soy sauce
2 tablespoons catsup
1 teaspoon sugar
Dash salt
1 tablespoon cornstarch dissolved into 2 tablespoons chicken
stock or cold water

Heat wok over high heat for 30 seconds. Pour in oil, heat for
about 30 seconds, reduce heat if it begins to smoke. Add the
ginger, garlic, green onions and cayenne. Stir fry 20 seconds,
then add shrimp. Cook until shrimp are pink and firm,
stirring constantly. Add the wine, soy, catsup, sugar and salt,
then stir. Stir cornstarch mixture to recombine it and add it to
the pan. Stir constantly until the mixture thickens and coats
the shrimp with a glaze. Serve with steamed rice.

Jerry "Jody" O'Keefe. Jr.

Stuffed Shrimp Capone

2 pounds jumbo fresh shrimp, peeled and deveined
1 cup Jody's stuffed crab mixture *(see p. 111)*
Seasoned flour/corn flour mixture to your taste

Pat crab mixture into the deveined shrimp, roll into the
seasoned flour. Fry until golden brown.

Jerry "Jody" O'Keefe , Jr.

Shrimp Casserole

1 10-ounce package yellow rice
1 pound fresh shrimp (peeled)
1 large onion
1 can Rotel tomatoes and chilis, chopped
½ bell pepper, chopped
1 can cream of mushroom soup
1 stick margarine

Optional:
1 small carton fresh mushrooms
(sliced and sauteed with bell pepper and onions)
4 slices American or Velveeta cheese

Cook yellow (saffron rice) according to directions on package. Saute onion and bell pepper with stick of margarine until onion is clear. Add remaining ingredients, bring to boil. Then simmer for 10 minutes. Put yellow rice in large casserole dish, pour shrimp mixture on top and mix together slightly. Place in preheated oven (350 degrees) and bake for 30 minutes.

Kathryn O'Keefe

Crawfish Cheese Tails

1 pound crawfish tails   1 tablespoon cayenne
1 tablespoon butter   1 teaspoon garlic powder
1 pint half and half cream   1 teaspoon salt
1 cup sliced mushrooms   2 bunches green onions, minced
1 large jar Cheese Whiz   1 teaspoon white pepper

Saute crawfish tails and mushrooms in butter. Add other ingredients. Serve over pasta, steaks or with bread as dip.

Mary O'Keefe Sumrall

Crawfish Fettucini

3 pounds crawfish tails
1 pound fettucini noodles
1½ cups butter
3 medium onions, finely chopped
2 medium bell peppers, finely chopped
¼ cup flour
4 tablespoons dried parsley
1 pint half & half cream
1 pound Velveeta cheese cut in small squares
2 cloves garlic, minced
2 teaspoons jalapenos, chopped
Black pepper
Red pepper
Salt
Parmesan cheese

Melt butter, add onions and bell pepper. Cook until tender 20 minutes. Add flour. Cover and cook 15 minutes. Stir frequently. Add parsley and crawfish. Cook covered 15 minutes. Stir frequently.

Add cream, cheese, jalapenos, garlic, salt and pepper. Cover and cook on low 30 minutes. Stir occasionally. Cook fettucini according to directions.

Mix crawfish mixture and noodles thoroughly. Pour into 2-3 quart greased casserole dish. Sprinkle top with parmesan cheese. Bake in preheated oven at 350 degrees for 15-20 minutes. Servings: 16.

Mercedes O'Keefe Huval

Shrimp Diavolo over Pasta

1 pound small or medium sized fresh shrimp
1 6-ounce carton fresh mushrooms
1 26-ounce jar Newman's Own Bandito Diavolo sauce
½ cup white flour
¼ cup olive oil
2 9-ounce packages fresh angel hair pasta
Parmesan cheese, freshly grated

Peel shrimp, place in 5-quart sauce pan. Clean and slice fresh mushrooms, add to shrimp. Add the jar of Newman's Own Bandito Diavolo sauce. Stir, bring mixture to boil. Reduce heat and simmer for approximately 15 minutes. Meanwhile, in a small frying pain, make a roux with the flour and olive oil. Mix the flour and oil together with wire whisk until smooth in texture.

Bring to boil over high heat. Reduce heat to medium and stir constantly until medium brown (approximately five minutes). Remove from stove and continue stirring for two minutes. Slowly add roux to shrimp, mushroom and sauce mixture. Simmer for 10 minutes.

Prepare angel hair pasta according to directions. Serve prepared sauce over the angel hair pasta and sprinkle with grated Parmesan cheese. (Serves 4).

This is another recipe I developed for the Paul Newman's cooking contest, again, no win, but one of my favorite "quick and easy" recipes to cook for company. This recipe also makes a quick and delicious courtbouillon ("Koo-bee-on"). Omit shrimp, prepare sauce and pour over red fish, amberjack, trigger fish or any fish of your choice and bake in 350-degree oven until bubbling. Serve with rice.

Kathryn O'Keefe

Shrimp Spaghetti

1 medium package vermicelli, cooked
1 ½ sticks butter   3 cloves garlic, pressed
1 medium onion, chopped   1 small can mushrooms
2 pounds fresh shrimp, peeled   ½ cup Parmesan cheese
Salt and black pepper   3 tablespoons parsley, minced
Red pepper

Sauté garlic and onion until onions are transparent. Add mushrooms and shrimp. Cook until shrimp are pink. Add Parmesan cheese and season to taste. Toss with vermicelli and add minced parsley. Serve with hot French bread.

Cecilia O'Keefe Neustrom

Angel Hair Seafood

½ cup butter
¼ cup olive oil
1 clove garlic, chopped
1 cup fresh mushrooms
1 pound shrimp
1 pound crabmeat
½ cup chopped green onions
¼ cup chopped parsley
½ cup Parmesan cheese
1½ cups half-and-half
Salt and pepper
1 8.5-ounce package of angel hair pasta
¼ cup sherry

Melt margarine and add olive oil—Saute garlic and mushrooms until tender. Add shrimp and cook until pink and tender. Add green onions, half and half, and Parmesan cheese. Blend well. Add ¼ cup sherry. Cook about 10 minutes. Add parsley and a little thickening (flour) if needed. Add crabmeat and parsley. Heat well and serve over Angel Hair pasta. Serves 8-10.

Lorelei Stroble

Parmesan Shrimp or Oysters

3 pounds peeled, deveined, butterflied shrimp (*the bigger, the better*) or 3 pints oysters
½ box unseasoned bread crumbs
½ cup Parmesan cheese
½ cup Romano cheese
3 teaspoons paprika
2 tablespoons black pepper
1 teaspoon garlic powder
2 sticks melted butter

Preheat oven to 400 degrees. Melt the butter in a medium size pot and turn heat off. Mix together remaining ingredients in a bowl, except seafood. Gradually add mixture to the pot of butter, stirring, until the butter is all absorbed. You want to finish with the consistency of a thick paste. Do not make the mixture too dry, if you do add more melted butter. (You can save any leftover mixture for later use, it makes a good coating for baking fish or chicken as is, without the butter).

Mold a very light layer of the mixture to each shrimp or oyster and lay them on an ungreased cookie sheet. Place the cookie sheet on the bottom rack in the oven. The cheeses, breadcrumbs and seasonings will become a well browned, firm coating, when this happens, gently turn the shrimp over and do likewise.

If you are doing this recipe with oysters, steep the oysters in a pot of very hot water until they are very well curled at their edges. Remove them, pat dry and apply the very light coating before baking. Note: You will notice that this recipe calls for no salt. This is not a mistake. The cheeses supply all of the salt necessary.

Jerry "Jody" O'Keefe, Jr.

Cecilia O'Keefe Neustrom preparing to get after a fresh oyster (c. 1992).

Oyster & Andouille Pie

1 9-inch pie shell
2 dozen oysters (reserve 1 cup oyster liquid)
2 finely chopped celery stalks
1 medium onion, finely chopped
1 bell pepper, finely chopped
3 bay leaves
3 cloves chopped garlic
3 tablespoons chopped parsley
8 ounces skinned & chopped andouille or other smoked sausage
¼ cup Italian bread crumbs
¼ cup oil and 3 tablespoons flour *(for a roux)*

Sauté vegetables, herbs and andouille in a little oil till tender. Add the oyster water and simmer for 10 minutes. In another pan combine oil and flour, cook, stirring till dark brown. Add the roux to the vegetables and stock, then simmer 5 minutes. Add the oysters and cook until oyster edges are curled. Fold in bread crumbs. Pour mixture into crust and bake 30 minutes or until crust is golden brown. Let stand 10 minutes in a warm spot before serving.   *Jerry "Jody"O'Keefe, Jr.*

Oysters A & M Breaux

Raw oysters
Butter
Lemon juice
Tony Chachere's seasoning
Waverly wafers, crackers of your choice
Tabasco

On a medium hot barbecue grill heat a cookie sheet. Lay some oysters on the sheet in a single layer. Cook until edges are curled. Pour off oyster juice - or at least most of it. Add enough butter to coat the oysters, let it melt. Sprinkle with seasonings to taste.

Take your wafers, one person at a time, no shoving or pushing and flip wafers in the butter sauce on the cookie sheet. Take an oyster or two for each wafer, place on the wafers and eat. Then you have to back off and let someone else have a chance at'em.

This recipe comes direct from the heart of Cajun Country, by Andrew and Myra Breaux of Houma, Louisiana - My great friends and companions, whether cooking, fishing or duck hunting!

Jerry "Jody" O'Keefe, Jr.

Sue's Italian Mussels

2 dozen mussels
½ cup olive oil
5 cloves garlic
Salt and pepper to taste

4-5 tablespoons oregano
1 tablespoon basil
1 can whole tomatoes

Steam mussels in colander over boiling water. Saute garlic in olive oil. Add canned tomatoes with juice. Season with remaining ingredients. Add mussels and cook covered for 10 minutes on medium heat. Serve with linguini pasta.

Sue Pitalo Jordan

Oysters Ambrosia

2 cups brown sauce, fairly thick (*see p. 156*)
1 cup of a good red wine
1½ cups oyster water (reduced to ½ cup)
5 bay leaves
1 tablespoon minced garlic
3 teaspoons Lea & Perrins Worcestershire sauce
8 ounces fresh lump crabmeat
4 green onions, diced
1½ dozen oysters
1½ cups flour
Oil for frying
Salt and pepper

Combine brown sauce, wine, oyster water, bay leaves and garlic. Cook 15 minutes on low heat. Add Lea & Perrins, crabmeat and green onions, cook 3 minutes on low. Keep sauce hot. Season and coat oysters in flour. Fry till golden brown. Stir oysters lightly in sauce mixture and serve. Good over pasta of any kind.

Jerry "Jody" O'Keefe, Jr.

BEEF, PORK & GAME

*Jeff O'Keefe (c. 1993) carving a roasted pork ham.
On holidays at the home of Jerry and Annette O'Keefe,
his parents, it's not uncommon to have between
two and three dozen guests for Sunday lunch.*

Favorite Roast Beef

12-15 pounds boneless chuck roast
12-15 garlic cloves, whole
1 cup Lea & Perrins Worcestershire sauce
Cayenne pepper
12-15 whole peeled potatoes
12-15 whole carrots
1 pint hot tomato relish
Paprika

Stuff roast with garlic. Pour Lea & Perrins over roast, then pack with tomato relish and sprinkle all over with cayenne. Surround with potatoes and carrots. Sprinkle them with salt, pepper and paprika. Pour in enough water to half cover vegetables.

Bake uncovered at 325 degrees for five to six hours. Crust should be carmelized when done. Note: This recipe can be used on outdoor barbeque. Wrap roast securely in heavy foil to keep juices in.

This has been an all-time favorite with the family. It came from a friend in Georgia and we adapted it to suit our needs. It is a marvelous treat for a crowd.

Rose Annette O'Keefe

Beef Brisket

1 large brisket   Dry mustard
Salt   Black and red pepper

Season well with salt and peppers. Rub with dry mustard. Marinate overnight. Roast eight hours at 325 degrees in uncovered pan. When done, let sit several hours, then slice very thin to serve.

Marinade:
1½ cup olive oil
½ cup fresh lemon juice
1 cup soy sauce
2 tablespoons dried parsley
2 tablespoons Lea & Perrins Worcestershire sauce
1 cup dry red wine
2 tablespoons dry yellow mustard

Used marinade may be stored in refrigerator for future use.

Sugar Roast

Chuck Roast 3-4 inches thick
Soy Sauce
Salt and pepper
Sugar

Soak roast in soy sauce. Salt and pepper on each side. Spread granulated sugar on all sides and sprinkle with soy sauce to help it stick. On hot charcoal fire, place roast directly over coals but not too close—if the fire flares too much, sprinkle with water. Cook approximately 15 minutes on each side (or a little longer if needed). Should be fairly charred on outside and rare on inside. *EAT!*

Dr. John B. O'Keefe

Barbecue Brisket or Roast

5-6 pounds brisket
½ bottle liquid smoke
Meat tenderizer
Celery salt

Garlic salt to taste
Onion salt to taste
4 tablespoons Lea & Perrins
8 ounces barbecue sauce

The day before serving, marinate by pouring liquid smoke over meat. Sprinkle with meat tenderizer, celery salt, onion salt and garlic salt. Cover with plastic wrap and refrigerate over night.

On serving day, sprinkle Worcestershire sauce over meat. Make tent of foil over pan and wrap tightly. Bake at 275 degrees for 5 hours. Uncover and pour barbecue sauce over meat. Replace uncovered meat in oven for 45 minutes. Remove meat to a platter and cover with foil for a few minutes to make cutting easier.

Ellen Parks Roche

Marinated Flank Steak

1 cup soy sauce
1 teaspoon ginger
1 clove garlic, finely chopped

2 bay leaves
1 teaspoon tarragon
3 ounces dry vermouth

Combine above ingredients and marinate steak for at least 2-4 hours. Cook on grill until medium rare. Slice on the diagonal across the grain.

Kathryn O'Keefe

Mongolian Barbecue

Vegetables:
1 cup minced ginger
1 cup bean sprouts
1 cup minced jalapenos
1 cup carrots sliced paper thin
1 cup chopped cabbage
1 cup sweet peppers sliced
1 cup chopped green onions
1 cup chopped white onions

Meats:
1 pound pork, cubed
1 pound turkey, cubed
1 pound beef, cubed
(any other meats you like, quantity according to crowd)

Sauces:

Soy sauce	Hot pepper oil
Vinegar and water	Shrimp oil
Sugar water	Sesame seed oil

Prepare vegetables, meats and sauces and place in separate containers. In two salad bowls select vegetables of your choice, then meats of your choice to which you add the sauces. Cook rapidly on hot grill or black skillet. Serve with rice.

Rose Annette O'Keefe

John O'Keefe, Michael Neustrom and David Huval (c. 1990), pulling
chef's duty at a family reunion held in Louisiana at the home of Kathryn O'Keefe.

Mardi Gras Cook Out

Some years ago, Jeff O'Keefe began a custom that has fast turned
into a tradition. As the parades roll past his home on Mardi Gras
day, family and friends congregate on his lawn near the street to see
what beads and trinkets they can catch. By his front porch, there
will be a huge tent with tables and chairs where Jeff barbeques
marvelous hot, spicy Hillshire Farm sausages and then places them
in a large roaster with more of the sauce. These are then put on
warm French bread buns to serve to the hungry crowd.

Inside his home, where the ladies and children can relax, the dining
table is loaded with various salads, cakes, cookies, chips and dips to
munch on. Jeff's wife Lynn is hostess throughout the day to many
who come and go during the three carnival parades. This is a
wonderful treat to enjoy.

Rose Annette O'Keefe

Barbecue Ribs

2 slabs pork ribs
1 cup salad oil
1 cup water
1 large onion chopped
4 cloves garlic, crushed
½ green pepper, chopped
¼ cup Worcestershire sauce
⅓ cup yellow mustard
1 tablespoon minced fresh ginger

6 lemons, juice and rind
1 teaspoon cayenne pepper
2 teaspoon black pepper
2 tablespoons paprika
2 tablespoons chili powder
2 teaspoons salt
2 cups ketchup

Saute onions, garlic and green pepper in oil until tender. Add remaining ingredients and simmer 1 hour. Lemons should be squeezed and the rind of three of the lemons sliced thin and added before cooking. While the sauce is simmering, coat ribs with season salt and set aside. Prepare charcoal and let coals get hot.

When hot, move coals all to one side of grill. Remove grill and place a pan of water on opposite side from coals. Place pecan wood or cracked pecan shells directly on coals. Return grill and place ribs over pan of water.

Cover grill and let ribs cook for 1½ hours, replenishing pecan wood as required. Add additional coals to fire. Coat ribs on both sides with sauce. Continue cooking for 1½ hours longer over medium heat. Recoat ribs every 20 minutes until done. Same recipe and procedure works well for chicken, just reduce cooking time by half. Recipe yields ½ gallon of sauce.

Chris Snyder

Glazed Beef Brisket

4 -5 pounds boneless beef brisket
1 large onion, quartered
10 -12 cloves
3 large garlic cloves, quartered
¾ teaspoon curry powder
4 bay leaves
4 finely chopped green onions
10 ounces currant jelly
 (*or your favorite flavor*)
⅓ cup white wine
4 tablespoons Zatarain's creole mustard (or Dijon)
Salt to taste
Fresh ground black pepper
½ teaspoon garlic salt

Trim all excess fat from brisket. Cover brisket, onion, garlic &
bay leaf with water in Dutch oven. Bring to boil, reduce heat
and simmer about 3 hours, until tender. Drain brisket, cover
and refrigerate overnight.

Combine jelly, wine, mustard, green onion, curry, garlic salt
in saucepan. Heat until jelly melts, salt & pepper to taste.
Place brisket in shallow roasting pan, brush with glaze. Cook
45 minutes at 325 degrees, basting often.

Jerry "Jody" O'Keefe, Jr.

Beef Tips Burgundy

16 pounds sirloin roast, cut in 1½ inch cubes
10 cloves garlic, minced
1 pound margarine or butter
4 cups cooking sherry
4 tablespoons dry mustard
1 tablespoon salt
1 tablespoon cayenne pepper
4 tablespoons Lea and Perrins Worcestershire sauce
1 tablespoon Tabasco or Louisiana hot sauce
2 pounds fresh mushrooms, sliced
2 tablespoons corn starch

In turkey roaster, brown meat in margarine. Add garlic, sherry, mushrooms and other seasonings. As meat juice increases in volume, mix water with corn starch and stir into mixture, allowing to thicken slightly. Cook at 350 degrees in oven until meat is done. Serve over parsley rice. Makes 20 servings or more.

One of my favorites for large group buffet dinners with steamed rice, rolls, salad platter with oil and vinegar dressing. Peas with pearl onions and mushrooms may also be served. Small chocolate and lemon tarts are nice for dessert with coffee.

Rose Annette O'Keefe

Top Round Pepper Steak

2 pounds top round steak, about 1 inch thick
3 tablespoons crushed peppercorns
2 tablespoons cognac
¼ cup red wine
Choppped parsley to taste
2 tablespoons butter
½ cup whipping cream
½ teaspoon garlic salt
2 tablespoons oil
Salt to taste

Mix peppercorns, butter and garlic salt. Press into both sides of steak. Heat oil in black iron skillet, medium high. Cook steak to desired amount (8 to 10 minutes). Remove steak to warm platter. Deglaze skillet with wine and cognac (high heat). Reduce heat, add cream, parsley and green onions. Cook 2 - 3 minutes, add salt to taste. Slice steak across grain diagonally in thin slices. Pour sauce over steak.

Jerry "Jody" O'Keefe, Jr.

Swiss Steak

2 round steaks	½ cup oil
1 cup flour	1 large onion sliced thin
2 teaspoons salt	4 cloves garlic, minced
2 teaspoons black pepper	2 cups water

Pound steaks with flour, salt and pepper, using wooden mallet or side of plate. Cut each steak into 6 pieces, brown on both sides in oil, using large skillet. Add garlic, onions and water, cover with tight lid and steam slowly five minutes or until steak is tender. Serve over steamed rice. Serves 10-12.

Rose Annette O'Keefe

Steak au Poivre

Peppercorn mixture:
Black, white, green, pink peppercorns and whole allspice
   (*crack in electric coffee/spice grinder or blender*)
Beef tenderloin (*filet mignon*)
1 small package fresh mushrooms
½ cup peanut oil
2 half pints heavy cream
2 ounces E & J Brandy
½ cup beef stock
2 sticks butter

Trim all fat from steaks. Press cracked peppercorns into steaks. Pour enough oil into bottom of pan to cover bottom. Brown steaks on all sides—remove from pan and place in oven on low. Pour any excess oil from pan.

Deglaze pan drippings with E&J brandy. Add all remaining ingredients. Cook until sauce reduces to half the original amount.

Return steaks to pan with sauce—coat with sauce. Heat plates in low temp oven. Serve steaks with generous amount of sauce and hot french bread. Serves 4-5 people.

Steak Bleu Cheese

3 large sirloins, 1 inch thick
6 ounces Bleu cheese, crumbled
Salt, pepper, Lea & Perrins Worcestershire sauce

Trim fat from outer edges of steak, nick every few inches through fat up to red meat to avoid steak curling. Spread heavily with crumbled bleu cheese, sprinkle lightly with salt, pepper and Worcestershire sauce. Place broiler pan on second rack down from broiler unit. Cook to medium rare stage. Do not turn over. Cut each sirloin into four pieces, serve piping hot.
This recipe is a sure winner!!

Rose Annette O'Keefe

Veal Cutlet Provolone

4 6-ounce veal cutlets   Lemon wedges
Juice of 1 lemon   ¼ bunch chopped parsley
5 tablespoons butter   Salt and pepper to taste
6 tablespoons Parmesan cheese
2 cups fine bread crumbs
2 eggs, beaten
2 tablespoons oil
4 ¼-inch slices of Provolone or Brie cheese

Pound cutlets very thin. Sprinkle both side with salt, pepper, lemon juice and parmesan cheese. Blend eggs, oil and parsley. Coat cutlets in mixture and then coat with bread crumbs. Sauté in butter until browned.

Place a slice of cheese on each, lower heat, cover skillet. Cook until cheese melts, garnish with lemon and serve. Note: This same recipe is very good with boneless chicken breasts also.

Jerry "Jody" O'Keefe, Jr.

Veal Marsala

2 tablespoons vegetable oil   ¼ cup chopped parsley
3 tablespoons butter   ⅓ cup heavy cream
1 pound thin veal   ½ cup dry Marsala
5 tablespoons flour spread on dish
Salt and pepper to taste

Heat oil and butter in a large skillet, dredge veal pieces in flour one at a time on both sides. Brown veal in skillet quickly on both sides. (Do not put any more than will fit without overlapping.) One minute or so on each side is sufficient.

Transfer to platter—do not overlap—use more than one platter if necessary. Continue cooking until all meat is done and has been transferred to platter. Season with salt and freshly ground pepper.

Add Marsala to pan, turning heat on high. Scrape cooking residues loose until deglazed. Add cream and stir constantly until juice and cream form a thick sauce. Turn heat to medium, put veal into sauce turning each piece to coat with sauce.

Transfer to heated serving platter and pour remaining sauce over all. Sprinkle with parsley and serve immediately. Serves 4.

Lorelei Stroble

Burrito Heaven

2 pounds lean ground beef
1 large onion, chopped
3 cloves garlic, minced
1 tablespoon of the best chili powder available
½ cup flour
1 tablespoon salt
   (your own seasoned salt formula will make it better)
1 tablespoon fresh ground black pepper
1 cup cold water
2 cans refried beans
1 dozen large tortillas
1 pound of grated sharp Cheddar cheese
1 jar Pace or Old El Paso Picante Sauce

In a black iron skillet, cook the hamburger, onion and garlic until done. Remove grease leaving two or three tablespoons in the skillet. Stir in the flour, chili powder, salt and pepper, mix well.

Add the water gradually while stirring. Bring the mixture to a slow boil. Reduce heat, partially cover and simmer for 30 minutes, stirring often.

Heat beans in a small pan. Warm tortillas in the oven or microwave. Spread one large spoon of beans and 2 spoons meat on each tortilla. Add cheese and picante sauce to taste, roll it up and eat it!

Jerry "Jody" O'Keefe, Jr.

Meat Loaf Mania

1½ pound ground beef
½ pound ground veal
½ pound ground pork
2 large onions, diced
2 bell pepper, diced
4 ribs celery, diced
½ cup green onion tops
  (chopped)
2 tablespoons dry mustard
1 small can tomato paste
½ pound bacon, crumbled
½ cup evaporated milk
1½ cups beef stock or bouillon

3 bay leaves
¾ cups cracker crumbs
2 eggs beaten
2 teaspoons basil
2 teaspoons salt
1 teaspoon black pepper
1 teaspoon garlic powder
1 teaspoon onion powder
3 teaspoons paprika

Preheat oven to 350 degrees. Fry bacon, remove from pan and crumble. Add onion and cook till golden brown (very important step). Add bell pepper and celery, cook until tender.

Add the tomato paste and cook while stirring about 3 - 4 minutes. Stir in the seasonings, bay leaf and beef stock. Remove bay leaf and put vegetable mixture into a mixing bowl. Stir in the evaporated milk and bacon.

Combine the beef, veal , pork, eggs and cracker crumbs in another bowl. Combine vegetable mixture to the meat mixture.

Place the mixture in a greased baking pan, form into loaf. Bake 45 minutes at 350 degrees.

Jerry "Jody" O'Keefe, Jr.

Canadian Meat Pies

2½ pounds pork
2½ pounds veal
1 large onion, chopped
5 teaspoons salt
1 teaspoon black pepper
2 teaspoons cinnamon
½ teaspoon cloves
½ teaspoon allspice

Rose Millette Brodeur

Grind pork and veal in a large pan. With a small amount of water, add in onion and spice ingredients. Cook for ½ hour. Let cool and then put in the refrigerator over night. For pies, sprinkle flour inside of the raw pie shells, put in meat mixture, cover with pie crust and put a slash through the top. Cook at 350 degrees for one hour. Yield: 5 or 6 pies.

Rose Millette "Moma Rose" Brodeur

This recipe was passed down from my French Canadian grandmother, "Moma Rose," to my mother and on to me. The spices are unusual and delightful.

Rose Annette O'Keefe

Meat Loaf

3 pounds ground chuck
1 large onion, minced
1 large bell pepper, minced
1 stalk celery, minced
½ bunch parsley, minced
1 can tomatoes, drained and chopped
3 cups corn flakes, crumbled
1 can evaporated milk
1 egg, beaten
Salt, pepper to taste (Worcestershire, catsup)

Combine all of above ingredients. Shape into loaf and place on rack in roaster pan. Put catsup and Worcestershire sauce on top of loaf to make pretty crust. Bake at 350 degrees. You may want to put 1 cup water under roasting rack to prevent drippings from sticking.

Rose Annette O'Keefe

Roasted Leg of Lamb

1 leg of lamb   Salt
12 cloves garlic   Red pepper
12 pieces fresh ginger   Paprika
3 cups sherry   3 cups soy sauce

Stuff lamb with garlic and ginger. Place in roaster, then pour wine and soy sauce over it. Rub salt, red pepper and paprika generously over leg of lamb. Add 3 cups warm water to roaster being careful not to wash off salt, red pepper and paprika. Roast at 325 degrees for 3-4 hours depending on how well done you like your roast.

Rose Annette O'Keefe

Grilled Leg of Lamb Dijon

1 large leg of lamb
2 jars Dijon mustard
2 tablespoons fresh ginger
4 cloves garlic
5 tablespoons soy sauce
1 teaspoon salt
1 tablespoon rosemary
1 teaspoon cayenne pepper
1 tablespoon thyme
5 tablespoons olive oil

Have butcher bone and butterfly leg of lamb. Remove any excess fat or membrane left on by butcher. The lamb should be as lean as possible. Blend together the next seven ingredients. Crush the garlic and finely chop fresh ginger and add to mixture.

Coat leg of lamb thoroughly and refrigerate over night in sealed container. Prepare coals and add pecan wood or cracked pecan shells prior to grilling. Grill over hot coals for 12-15 minutes on each side.

Chris Snyder

This is the piéce de résistance at the traditional family Easter fest held at the Snyder home in Ocean Springs, Mississippi. You won't find a morsel left when the meal is done; that can't be said for other meat dishes.

Rose Annette O'Keefe

Barbecue Lamb Loins

2 pounds boneless lamb loin	Salt
⅔ cup yogurt	Black Pepper
4 cloves garlic, minced	Cayenne Pepper
1 tablespoon basil leaves	1 teaspoon tumeric
½ teaspoon ginger	1 teaspoon cumin

Mix seasonings together. Marinate in large zip lock bag overnight. Grill on medium hot grill, approximately 5 minutes each side for medium rare. Slice into ½ inch thick slices for serving. Add ⅓ cup yogurt to marinade for serving sauce.

Jerry "Jody" O'Keefe, Jr.

Venison & Gravy

3 - 4 pounds venison	Salt to taste
(back strap if available)	Black pepper to taste
Flour	Cayenne pepper to taste
Oil	Paprika to taste
2 cloves garlic, diced	4 tablespoons Lea & Perrins
1 large onion diced	1 cup red wine
1 large bell pepper, diced	Juice of 2 lemons

Cut meat into 2 inch cubes. Mix lemon juice, wine, Lea & Perrins and seasonings together (*taste it, if it isn't just right play around with it - don't be afraid to experiment*). Marinate overnight in a covered dish or plastic bag. Drain marinade and set aside for later use.

Roll venison in flour and shake off excess. Brown in oil in a Dutch Oven, add vegetables and cook till lightly browned. Add reserved marinade, cover and cook on low about 2 hours, stir often. Serve as is or over rice. Note: This marinade and method is also great with beef shishkabobs or wild duck.

Jerry "Jody" O'Keefe, Jr.

Rabbit Stew

(for non-game eaters, substitute round steak/veal/pot roast)
2 skinned and quartered rabbits
1 bunch carrots, cleaned & cut as you please
1 pound new potatoes, peeled & halved
2 large onions, chopped
½ bunch celery, chopped
2 bell peppers, chopped
1 small can tomato paste
1 large can whole skinned tomatoes, chopped
2 cups beef stock (or beef bouillon)
1 cup red wine
Salt, red, white & black pepper to taste
1 teaspoon Lea & Perrins Worcestershire sauce

Boil potatoes in salted water until ⅓ done (test with fork).

Brown rabbit pieces in a Dutch oven, add remaining ingredients, simmer covered 1 hour, remove meat and debone. Adjust seasonings, add deboned meat and simmer uncovered until stew is desired consistency (usually 45 minutes or so).

Serve in a bowl over a little rice. Note: By adjusting cooking times to suit the meat, this same recipe is suited very well for dove, duck, goose, venison, or your favorite beef cut.

Jerry "Jody" O'Keefe, Jr.

Roasted Wild Duck (or Venison)

1 dozen ducks, cleaned well of pin feathers
1 dozen small onions
1 dozen stalks celery
1 dozen cloves garlic
1 pound margarine, melted
Salt, black and red pepper
½ gallon Burgundy wine

Heat oven to 400 degrees. Stuff each duck with onion, celery and garlic pieces. Sprinkle cavity generously with salt, black and red pepper. Rub skin with margarine.

Place ducks, breast side down, in large roaster, pour remaining melted margarine over. Then add burgundy wine which should almost cover ducks. Place roaster in oven and reduce heat to 325 degrees. Cook slowly, baste occasionally until done. Serve with wild rice.

Excellent for a "bachelor" dinner after the hunt; this recipe is bound to please your man. Note: Some people "swear by rare" ducks. We like ours well done. And the same seasonings given above work fine for roasting venison, chopping onions, celery and garlic to put over roast.

Rose Annette O'Keefe

Captain Jody's Baked Dove or Duck

This recipe requires 3 steps to reach the final delight.

2 dozen dove breasts, skinned
or 8 duck breasts, skinned

(Step 1) Mirepoix

2 carrots, diced	Madeira wine
1 large onion, diced	2 tablespoons butter
2 celery heart, diced	1 slice bacon, minced
1 bay leaf, crushed	¼ teaspoon thyme

Sauté the vegetables in the butter until soft. Deglaze pan with Madeira. You should have about 1½ cups of seasonings. Set aside to use later, in Step 2.

(Step 2) Brown Sauce
½ cup beef or veal fat, minced
½ cup flour
12 black peppercorns
2 small cans tomato puree
½ bunch parsley, coarsely chopped
10 cups beef stock

In a heavy skillet melt the fat and add the cooked vegetables from Step 1. Add the flour and stir until medium dark browned. Stir in remaining ingredients except stock, mix well. Add stock and simmer 2-3 hours until reduced by ½. Strain stock and set aside to cool.

You now have what is known in French cookery as a Brown Sauce. This is a very versatile sauce and can be used in many other recipes. You will need only 2 cups of it to complete this recipe, so when it cools, freeze the remainder in ice trays or preserve in baggies for later use. A time saver.

(continued on next page)

Capt. Jody's Dove or Duck (cont'd)

(Step 3)
2 cups brown sauce
1 small white onion, minced
4 tablespoons butter
2 cups sliced mushrooms
½ cup dry white wine
1 cup tomato sauce
2 teaspoons chopped parsley
2 tablespoons Lea & Perrins
Salt and pepper to taste

Preheat oven to 325 degrees. Sauté onion in the butter until tender. Stir in the mushrooms and sauté 2 minutes. Add the wine and simmer until reduced by ½. Add remaining ingredients, simmer for 10 minutes. Correct seasonings.

Score the breasts of the birds lightly, dredge in seasoned flour and brown in bacon fat or oil. Place in a baking dish, pour sauce over breasts and bake until tender. Test with a fork for doneness. About 45 minutes to 1 hour cooking time. Serve over wild rice or pasta with plenty sauce.

An effort, but worth it. One of the best dishes ever cooked, (according to Jody).

Jerry "Jody" O'Keefe, Jr.

Duck Sauce Picante

2 large ducks
1 cup brown rice
1 cup flour
1 cup oil
2 cans of large, whole tomatoes
1 bulb garlic
2 large onions

2 large sweet peppers
Bay leaves
Cayenne Pepper
Basil
Oregano
Salt

Make a roux, mixing and browning slowly the oil and flour. Set aside to cool. Dice entire bulb of garlic, onions and bell peppers and dump them into a big pot along with two cans of whole tomatoes. Add the roux to the pot and about a quart of water. Bring to a boil on high, then turn back to a simmer.

Skinning the ducks is optional. Some people prefer the skin on for more of the wild flavor (if they're wild). Either way, cut each duck into 8 pieces: two legs, two halves of breast, and two halves of the back. Put all the pieces into the pot.

Add five or six bay leaves. Sprinkle enough salt and red pepper to lightly dust the top of the mixture, then stir it in (add more for a hotter style). Add a dash of basil and oregano. Then let the whole mixture simmer for as long as it takes you to go to the latest movie you've been itching to see.

Cook one cup of brown rice, adding a tablespoon of oil to the rice to keep it from sticking. (Two cups of water). Serve the duck over rice in bowls or on plates. The mixture can be made thicker if you want, by cooking it longer; or it can be made thinner, by adding more water. Again, this is a matter of personal preference. Serves 8 to 10 people easy.

John Michael O'Keefe, Sr.

Roasted Pork Ham

15-18 pound pork rump roast or fresh pork ham
1 whole head garlic
Fresh ginger cut in small pieces
1 small can dried yellow mustard
Salt and red pepper as needed to coat roast
Paprika to cover roast
3 cups soy sauce

Remove skin from roast and punch holes all over. Stuff holes with garlic and ginger. Rub all over with dried mustard, then coat roast with salt, red pepper and paprika last of all. This will make a beautiful crust. Place dressed meat in large roaster with 3-4 cups warm water and soy sauce. Set oven at 325 degrees, roast meat 6-8 hours until well done.

In addition to roasted turkey, this fresh pork ham is always a favorite at Christmas and Thanksgiving. For an extra treat, scrape fat from skin that was removed. Cut in 2 inch squares, roast in oven also until real crispy. These are called "cracklings" and make a wonderful snack to nibble while roast cooks and makes your mouth water.

Rose Annette O'Keefe

Boneless Pork Loin

2 pounds boneless pork loin
1 cup sherry
1 cup soy sauce
  (used as salt substitute)
½ cup olive oil
1 tablespoon red pepper
2 tablespoons garlic powder
2 tablespoons ginger (ground)

Slice pork in thick medallions. Marinate in sherry, soy sauce, ginger, garlic and red pepper. Heat wok to high temperature. Add olive oil to coat bottom and sides of wok. Place medallions of pork flat side down, brown thoroughly then turn. Reduce heat to medium low, add remainder of marinade and simmer a few minutes longer. This is delicious with steamed rice or angel hair pasta. Serves 6-8 people. Note: Boneless chicken breasts work well with these ingredients and prepared the same way.

Rose Annette O'Keefe

Florence's Pork Ribs

6 racks ribs, cut apart
1 cup cornstarch, moistened with water
½ gallon sherry
½ cup cider vinegar
2 cups soy sauce
2 tablespoons brown sugar
½ cup grated ginger
1 tablespoon red pepper
6 cloves garlic, minced

Put all of above in large pot and heat to boiling and until cornstarch thickens gravy. Add cut up ribs and turn low to simmer, cooking gently 30-40 minutes until meat is tender and wants to pull loose from bones.

This recipe is unusual and authentic Hawaiian.

Florence Pettis

Stuffed Pork Roast

1 18-pound fresh pork rump roast, skin on
2 large onions, halved then sliced
1 bunch green onions, chopped
1 whole head garlic, peeled and minced
½ cup minced parsley
⅓ cup vinegar
1 tablespoon season-all
2 tablespoon salt
1 tablespoon black or red pepper

Combine above ingredients and use mixture to stuff roast, packing as much in as possible from both ends.

You may want to have butcher cut two nice pockets down the bone of roast. If you prefer to do it yourself, use a long thin bladed knife, insert at end of roast, twist blade to enlarge pocket at center. Repeat process at other end of roast.

Put roast in heavy foil, pour rest of mixture on roast, seal foil with drug store wrap, place in roaster and bake in oven at 275 degrees for 3-4 hours. After 2½ hours unseal foil to allow roast to brown for remainder of time. Use meat thermometer to tell when well done.

Hazel Pitalo

This makes a wonderful feast at Christmas or Thanksgiving—especially good in cold weather. Count on a happy crowd when serving. Thanks to George & Hazel Pitalo for this treat!!
Rose Annette O'Keefe

Stuffed Ham

Whole Ham	Sugar
Water	1 cup vinegar
1 whole apple	1 whole onion

Put whole ham in pan with water to cover. To water add apple, onion and ½ cup vinegar. Simmer until ham can be pierced with sharp pick. Cook in liquid.

Lift out, turn fat side up, split lengthwise and remove bone. Put stuffing in cavity. Tie in shape, set in roasting pan, fat side up. Sprinkle sugar on top. Pour ½ cup vinegar in pan and bake 1½ hours in medium oven to brown. Serve cold, sliced thin, with fruit salad, hot biscuits and beverage.

Dressing:

1 cup bread crumbs	2 raw eggs
1 teaspoon dry mustard	1 cup chopped parsley
1 teaspoon celery seed	1 small chopped onion
1 teaspoon pepper	½ teaspoon red pepper
2 tablespoons brown sugar	2 tablespoons vinegar

Caroline B. Sasser

Caroline B. Sasser, or "Aunt Caro," was my mother's youngest sister and a wonderful cook. She also passed many recipes to us that we treasure.

Rose Annette O'Keefe

Fourth of July Chili and Dogs

For over 25 years our entire family, with friends included, took an all day boat trip on the Sea Queen with Captain Ralph Baker and his "First Mate" Bernice. We would fish, by trolling, all the way to our destination, Horn Island, where we spent the day, primarily swimming and eating. In addition to Florence's Fried Chicken, we always had a huge pot of chili and hot dogs. Here it is—

9 pounds ground beef
6 large onions, minced
2 large sweet peppers, minced
4 cloves garlic, minced
3 cans kidney beans (*optional*)
3 large cans crushed tomatoes
1 large can tomato paste
½ cup Lea & Perrins
4 tablespoons red pepper
6 tablespoons chili powder

On medium heat brown, stir and saute ground beef, onions, sweet pepper and garlic until well done. Add tomatoes, tomato paste, chili powder, salt, red pepper and ½ cup Lea &

Chili and Dogs (cont'd)

Perrins Worcestershire sauce, mixing thoroughly. Cook for additional hour, add water if necessary.

Mix several packs of whole hot dogs in meat mixture to heat before serving. Serve as chili dogs with mustard and chopped onions on buns, or serve in a bowl with crackers to accompany. Makes enough chili for 6 packs of hot dogs.

Great for a crowd of hungry kids on the water!!

Rose Annette O'Keefe

POULTRY

*Rose Annette O'Keefe (c.1993), shown here
in the kitchen of her home in Biloxi, Mississippi. Over the years,
the virtually non-stop traffic of children and friends through
the kitchen of the O'Keefe home made it a familial Grand Central
Station of impromptu feasts, reunions, political debate, argument,
departures, revelry and announcements.*

Nicki's Baked Turkey

1 large turkey 20-24 pounds
Salt
Black Pepper
2 large onions, peeled and quartered
2 stalks celery, cut in half crosswise
1 stick margarine or 1 cup oil
2 quarts warm water
Paprika

Remove giblets from cavities of turkey and boil in water with salt and pepper. When very tender, remove meat from neck bone and dice gizzard and liver. Use either for turkey dressing or gravy.

Salt and pepper cavities of bird and stuff with onions and celery. Rub skin of turkey either with margarine or oil.

Place bird in large roaster, breast side up with legs trussed, and add water to pan. Sprinkle lightly with paprika to come out golden brown. Put a tent of foil over bird but do not tuck edges.

Roast at 325 degrees six to eight hours. At very last, baste bird with juices, and salt and pepper outside skin. When cool, slice with electric knife.

Nicki O'Keefe

This method produces very juicy meat due to slow cooking—very, very good!! Best turkey ever and sure to get raves!

Rose Annette O'Keefe

Moma's Turkey Dressing Canadian Style

2 batches corn bread, standard box recipe
1 loaf stale French bread, or toasted fresh
3 onions, minced
2 sweet bell peppers, minced
4 stalks celery, minced
1 bunch parsley, minced
2 bunches green onions, minced
Turkey giblets, cooked and minced
6 large eggs
Turkey broth or canned chicken consomme
2 tablespoons cinnamon
1 tablespoon nutmeg
2 teaspoons allspice
2 teaspoons ground cloves
1 tablespoon salt
1 tablespoon black pepper
1 stick margarine
Paprika

Make corn bread according to box recipe, cool and crumb into very large bowl. Soak French bread in water, squeeze dry and crumble; add to corn bread. Add all of chopped vegetables, giblets and crack eggs over mixture; add turkey broth or consomme to moisten.

Sprinkle spices over all. Toss until well blended, put in large baking pan, dot with margarine and sprinkle with paprika to make pretty and brown. Bake at 350 degrees until well done, 30-40 minutes. Dressing should be moist inside with crust all over. Serves 30-40.

Recipe handed down through generations, from Moma Rose to Ceci Saxon to Rose Annette O'Keefe.

Fried Turkey

A recipe concocted out of the swamps of south Louisiana. You get a few Cajuns around a pot of hot oil and something's going to get put in it.

1 whole turkey
1 jar Cajun injector marinade for poultry
1½ cups mustard
Tony Chachere's creole seasoning
4-5 gallons peanut oil
Crawfish pot & boiler
Cooking thermometer

The night before you cook this bird you want to have him thawed out sufficiently to inject the marinade, and if you like a little extra spice you can add a little Tony Chachere's creole seasoning to the marinade. Inject the turkey in all its major meat areas. Take the mustard in your fingers and cover the turkey thoroughly. Then sprinkle some Tony Chachere's on to the bird. Cover and leave in the refrigerator over night.

Place enough oil in the pot to submerge the turkey completely. Important: do not let the oil exceed 375 degrees. As a rule of thumb, cook the turkey for 4 minutes per pound. Most turkeys cook for approximately 1 hour. Sometimes the wings get overcooked because the size of the bird requires a longer cooking time. You may want to cut off the wings and add them to the oil later in the cooking process.

Jeff O'Keefe

Waiting impatiently . . . to ensure a fair start of the annual Easter egg hunt, grandchildren are required to wait on the front steps of Susan and Chris Snyder's home in Ocean Springs. The Victorian-era house was previously owned by Mrs. Ceci Saxon, who had purchased it from the O'Keefe family. It was at that time that pre-teen Rose Annette Saxon first met the boy who would later become her husband, Jerry O'Keefe.

Easter Time at the Snyders

Come Easter Sunday, the O'Keefe clan gathers in Ocean Springs with Chris and Susan O'Keefe Snyder for the traditional Easter egg hunt and a tremendous feast to follow for the young and the old. Chef Chris marinates and smokes a beautiful butterflied leg of lamb. He has also barbeques a large fresh pork ham and maybe a turkey or roast beef. In addition to these wonderful meats, Susan always serves fresh asparagus spears, cornbread dressing, rice and gravy. Chris has taken over the minced oyster recipe that Aunt Mary began. Virginia brings the fresh stewed corn. There is a large platter of fresh veggies, pickles, black and green olives, and artichokes to nibble on. The desserts may include strawberry shortcake, New York-style cheesecake, chocolate and cream-filled creampuffs, and fresh strawberries for those watching the calories. You will find many of these recipes throughout the book. You'll want to try them again and again.

Rose Annette O'Keefe

Grandpa's Fried Chicken

8-10 fryers
1 box of salt
1 box of black pepper
5 pounds all purpose flour
2 gallons Mazola cooking oil
1 dozen brown grocery paper bags

Our chef is very particular and likes to cut up his own chickens. He first cuts off the wings as close to the breast as possible. Next he spreads open the leg and second joint and cuts almost to the back. He then separates the breast from the back on each side and removes to make four pieces, splitting down the center and then across each section. He also cuts the back into four sections, as many like to chew the bony pieces. Then the chicken pieces are put into two large pots with ice cubes, water and salt and refrigerated overnight.

The next morning our chef heats the oil in a large commercial double-sized cooker. While doing this, he pats the moisture dry with towels and salts and peppers each piece of chicken individually, before dredging in a roaster pan of flour.

When the indicator light shows the oil is ready, Chef Grandpa puts five or six pieces of prepared chicken into each of two baskets and lowers gently into the sizzling hot oil. He shakes and moves the pieces about as it cooks, removing when it is golden brown and done through and through (about 10-12 minutes). Large cookie sheets, containing brown paper bags for draining, are used to put chicken into warm oven with the door cracked. This keeps the chicken crispy. He changes the bags as needed to absorb most of the oil.

Then it is "come and get it for tasting and testing!" The necks and giblets serve as appetizers for those who can't wait.
This recipe is a favorite with the grandkids. No one can do it like Grandpa!!!

Rose Annette O'Keefe

Moma's Fricassee Chicken

2 fryers, cut up
2 cups olive oil or 2 sticks margarine
2 cups flour
2 large onions, minced fine
1 large sweet pepper, minced fine
2 stalks celery, minced
½ bunch parsley, minced
2 bunches green onions, minced
6 cloves garlic, minced
1 large tomato, chopped (*optional*)
Seasonings to taste: salt, red and black pepper
3 quarts warm water
2 teaspoon Kitchen Bouquet for color and flavor
1 can tomatoes, crushed (*optional*)

Salt and pepper pieces of chicken. In large pot brown the chicken, skin side down, in oil or margarine; remove from pot. Add flour to oil to make roux, stirring constantly not to burn. Add chopped vegetables, saute in roux for few minutes, then replace chicken to ingredients. Add seasonings, then pour in warm water slowly to make light gravy from roux mixture. Simmer until chicken is tender (not to fall from bone). Serve over steamed rice. Serves 10-12.

Rose Annette O'Keefe

Chicken, Hunter's Style

1 broiler-fryer, quartered (*about 3 pounds*)
1 tablespoon vegetable oil
1 tablespoon butter or margarine
¼ pound canned mushrooms
2 large canned tomatoes, chopped and some of the juice
¼ cup sliced green onions
1 garlic clove, crushed
¾ cup water
2 tablespoons lemon juice
1 teaspoon ground thyme or crumbled
1 teaspoon salt
⅛ teaspoon pepper
1 teaspoon cornstarch

Brown chicken in oil and butter in large skillet with a cover.

Add mushrooms, tomatoes, green onions, garlic, ½ cup of the water, lemon juice, thyme, salt and pepper. Cover and simmer five minutes or until chicken is tender. Remove chicken to a heated platter and keep hot. Makes 4 servings.

Blend cornstarch with remaining water. Stir into liquid in skillet. Cook, stirring until mixture thickens and bubbles (three minutes). Pour over chicken. Serve at once.

Maureen O'Keefe Ward

Mert's Cajun Chicken Spaghetti

1 chopped onion
1 chopped bell pepper
½ stick butter or margarine
1 can spanish style (Rotel) tomatoes
1 pound Velveeta cheese (chunks)
1 chicken* - boiled and deboned
Broth from boiled chicken
1 medium sized bag of spaghetti

Saute onions and bell pepper for 15 minutes (or until soft). Add can of Rotel and Velveeta cheese. Mix well and stir frequently until all cheese is melted. Add chicken to Rotel and cheese mixture. Mix well.

Boil spaghetti noodles in chicken broth. Drain noodles and add to mixture. Pour into casserole dish. Bake in oven for 15 minutes at 300 degrees. *May substitute boneless chicken breasts for whole chicken.

Mercedes O'Keefe Huval

Chicken & Dumplings

2 fryers, quartered
2 tablespoons salt
3 tablespoons black pepper
2 sticks butter

5 cups flour
2 cups Crisco shortening
1 cup water

In a pot cover quartered chickens with water and bring to a boil. Add the salt, pepper and butter. Reduce heat and slowly boil while preparing dumplings. In a mixing bowl place flour and work in shortening with a fork. Continue adding shortening, mixing well until the flour has a crumbly texture. Then begin kneading in cold water, a little at a time until the entire mixture has a smooth even texture and does not stick to your fingers.

Roll out pieces of the dough on a floured surface very, very thin (like thin noodles) then cut into long thin strips about ¼ inch wide. Place strips on a plate, cover with wax paper and roll and cut the rest likewise, alternating layers of dumplings and wax paper. Do not shake off excess flour.

Remove chicken from the stock and cool under running water, debone when cool. Bring stock to a rolling boil and begin adding dumpling strips, one or two at a time. Don't continue to add more until the water is boiling again and the added strips are floating at the top, otherwise they will stick to the bottom and burn. When all of the dumplings have been added, continue to boil for about 5 minutes. Taste a few for doneness - should taste just like noodles, not mushy.

Add the deboned chicken, correct seasonings, heat well while stirring the bottom and serve. If it needs thickening add a little cornstarch/water mixture to get your desired consistency. Serve in a bowl or on a plate. Good with a green salad. Note: When reheating, add a little more water to prevent sticking, use a double boiler, or reheat it in the microwave.   *Jerry "Jody" O'Keefe, Jr.*

Jerry "Jody" O'Keefe, Jr.

Chicken Picante

¼ cup medium hot chunky taco sauce
¼ cup Dijon mustard
2 tablespoons fresh lime juice
1 tablespoon fresh lemon juice
6 boneless, skinless chicken breast halves
4 tablespoons butter
6 tablespoons plain yogurt
1 lime cut into 6 segments

Mix taco sauce, mustard, lime juice and lemon juice in a large bowl. Marinate breasts at least 30 minutes. Remove breasts and fry in butter until brown. Add marinade and cook until breasts are done (5 minutes). Remove chicken to heated platter. Raise heat to high and boil marinade 1 minute. Pour over chicken, place 1 tablespoon yogurt and slice of lime on each.

Jerry "Jody" O'Keefe., Jr.

Easy Chicken Divan

3 boned chicken breasts
2 10-ounce packages of chopped broccoli
2 cans cream of chicken soup
¾ cup mayonnaise
1 tablespoon melted butter
½ cup sharp cheese, shredded
½ cup soft bread crumbs
½ teaspoon curry powder
1 teaspoon lemon juice

Cook broccoli in boiling water til tender. Drain well. Cook and slice chicken. Arrange broccoli in baking dish, oblong (9 x 13 or 7 x 11). Place chicken on top. Mix soup, mayonnaise, lemon juice, and curry powder. Pour over chicken and broccoli. Cover with cheese. Top with bread crumbs and butter. Bake at 350 degrees for 25-30 minutes or until hot.

Annette Longeway O'Keefe

Justin O'Keefe (c. 1991), working on a Cajun fried turkey, out by the garage in Biloxi. He has kept alive many of the family recipes, especially wonderful treats such as homemade caramels.

Maureen's Chicken Dijonnaise

1 chicken, cut up
¼ cup butter or oil
4 cups mushrooms, quartered
1 onion sliced in rings (or sliced green onions)
1 clove garlic, minced
1 cup water
1 teaspoon chicken stock base
1 teaspoon Dijon mustard
1 teaspoon salt or salt substitute
¼ teaspoon rosemary, crumbled

Saute chicken pieces in butter until browned on all sides. Remove chicken. In same pan, saute mushrooms, onions, and garlic. Drain excess fat. Stir into pan water, stock, mustard, salt and rosemary. Return chicken, cover skillet and simmer for 30 minutes. Note: 1 cup of chicken stock may be substituted for the water and chicken stock base.

Maureen O'Keefe Ward

Chicken Piccata

4 whole chicken breasts, skinned, boned and halved
½ cup flour
1½ teaspoons salt
¼ teaspoon freshly ground pepper
2 teaspoons paprika
¼ cup clarified butter
1 tablespoon olive oil
2-4 tablespoons dry Madeira or water
3 tablespoons fresh lemon juice
8 lemon slices
3-4 tablespoons capers (*optional*)
¼ cup minced fresh parsley (*optional*)

Place chicken breasts between two sheets wax paper and pound them until thin (¼ inch). Combine flour, salt, pepper, and paprika. Add breasts and coat well. Shake off excess.

Heat butter and olive oil in large skilled until bubbling. Saute chicken breasts, a few at a time, 2-3 minutes on each side. Do Not Overcook. Drain on paper towels and keep warm.

Drain off all but 2 tablespoons of butter and oil. Stir Madeira or water into drippings, scrape bottom of skilled to loosen any browned bits. Add lemon juice and heat briefly. Return chicken to skillet, top with lemon slices, and heat until sauce thickens. Add capers, sprinkle with minced parsley and serve. Makes 4-8 servings.

Mary O'Keefe Sumrall

Chicken Fajitas

16 boneless, skinless chicken breasts
1 large bottle of Wishbone Italian salad dressing
1 medium-size can of refried beans or black bean dip
1 pint sour cream
2 cups grated Cheddar or Monterey Jack cheese
2 cups shredded lettuce
2 cups tomatoes
2 cups guacamole
2 cups salsa
2 cups black olives
2 cups jalapeno or pepperoni peppers
2 jars artichoke hearts
16 medium-sized flour tortillas

Marinate 16 boneless, skinless chicken breasts at least three hours in advance or, preferably, a day ahead of time in Italian dressing mixed with any combination of your favorite seasonings.

Chop and/or prepare as many of the ingredients listed above as you wish. Serve in separate bowls.

Wrap 16 medium-size flour tortillas together in foil and heat in 350-degree oven for 30 minutes. Grill chicken breasts until done. Slice lengthwise into ¼" strips. Serve chicken, hot flour tortillas and condiments. Everyone creates their own fajita.

This is one of my favorite recipes to serve to a group of friends because almost everything is prepared ahead of time and after the chicken is grilled, everyone gets to help themselves and create their own fajita.

Kathryn O'Keefe

Pollo Flautas

3 tablespoons oleo
¼ cup flour
¼ teaspoon salt
1 cup chicken broth
2 tablespoons fresh chopped parsley
2 tablespoons lemon juice
2 teaspoons grated onion
1 dash paprika
1 dash nutmeg
1½ cups finely diced chicken (4 breasts)
12-14 flour tortillas

Avocado Sauce:
1 very ripe avocado
½ cup grated onion
Juice of 1 lemon

Melt oleo in skillet. Add flour and salt. Cook until thickened. Add chicken broth, parsley, lemon juice, onion, paprika, nutmeg and chicken. Cook until chicken is done.

Make avocado sauce by mashing avocado, adding ½ cup grated onion and juice of 1 lemon.

Place 1 tablespoon chicken mixture on each of 12-14 flour tortillas. Roll tightly and secure with toothpicks. Fry in hot oil at 350 degrees for 1-2 minutes. Top with avocado sauce.

Maureen O'Keefe Ward

MISCELLANEOUS

*"Daddy Ben" O'Keefe, introducing his granddaughter Maureen
to the pleasures of a good cigar (c. 1945?). He was a tall, handsome,
portly man who always had a cigar in his mouth. Sometimes he seemed
gruff, but for the most part he had a genial sense of humor and loved to
play practical jokes on his friends. He turned out to be a most generous
man as a father-in-law and was very good to me, although he teased me a
lot, especially about the kind of hats I liked to wear.*

Rose Annette O'Keefe

Wanda's Pizza

2 cups flour
1 package yeast
1 cup (8 ounces) warm water

½ teaspoon salt
1 tablespoon olive oil

Mix above and knead dough 8-10 minutes. Place in large wooden bowl, grease lightly with olive oil, cover with damp cloth and allow to rise in a warm place two hours.

After dough has risen, sprinkle with more flour, punch dough down and knead a few more minutes. Then you are ready to begin. Put the dough in the center of a large pan. Begin to spread with heel of your hand, working evenly from center out to edges until dough is desired thickness.

There are many toppings, but Wanda taught me to use this one:

1 can drained crushed tomatoes
½ pound grated Mozzarella cheese
1 package sliced pepperoni to cover top
1 teaspoon oregano flakes sprinkled over all
1 cup Parmesan or Romano cheese spread over all

Bake at 500 degrees until edges nice and brown.

Wanda Fremin

Many years ago, long before the pizza craze reached America, my friend Wanda Fremin from Naples, Italy, introduced us to pizza. She came to our home to show us "how Moma made it." As she used her ingredients, I would back track to measure the quantities. This is how it came out for one large or two small pizzas.

Rose Annette O'Keefe

Wanda's Fried Pizza

Using the same ingredients for the pizza dough noted in the previous recipe, add ½ cup more warm water to make a softer more elastic dough. Knead and let rise as before.

During the time the dough is rising, make this sauce.

2 pieces garlic, saute until brown then remove
½ cup olive oil
2 cups crushed tomatoes
1 tablespoon fresh basil or 1 teaspoon dried basil

Simmer sauce ½ to 1 hour, until it thickens. Now when dough rises, cut or break off small pieces and spread out with fingers. Deep fry dough in 2 cups cooking oil. It will puff up and get golden brown. Drain these pieces on paper towels, place on warm platter and spread 1-2 tablespoons of tomato sauce over each piece. Sprinkle with lots of romano cheese.

Wanda Fremin

Wanda gave me this version as a special recipe for this cookbook.
Rose Annette O'Keefe

Tomato Gravy for St. Joseph's Day

10 minced onions
1 large bunch celery, minced
5 large sweet peppers, minced
2 cups cooking oil
4 gallons tomato sauce
4 tablespoons salt
2 tablespoons black pepper

2 tablespoons sweet basil
2 tablespoons oregano
2 tablespoons fennel seeds
1 bottle Italian herbs
2 cups sardine mixture
2 tablespoons red pepper

Saute onions, celery and sweet peppers in oil. Add the rest of the ingredients. Cook slowly and stir frequently for several hours. If stored overnight, cool pot of sauce in the sink, changing water frequently. Note: sardine mixture is available in Italian specialty groceries. Yield: 50 to 75 servings.

This is a good all-around tomato gravy that is ideal for feeding a large crowd, for example a St. Joseph's Day gathering. Use this for meat balls and spaghetti, or for meat sauce with ground beef, or for baked fish courtbouillon. It is also good for shrimp spaghetti or chicken and spaghetti.

Rose Annette O'Keefe

Black Bean Spaghetti

1 large onion, sliced
1 small sweet red pepper, cut into strips
1 small sweet yellow pepper, cut into strips
1 8-ounce package fresh mushrooms, sliced
2 tablespoons olive oil
1 16-ounce can whole tomatoes, undrained and chopped
1 15-ounce can black beans, drained and rinsed
1 15-ounce can kidney beans, undrained
1 3-ounce jar of capers, drain off ½ of liquid
¼ cup sliced, ripe olives
¼ teaspoon dried rosemary
¼ teaspoon dried basil
¼ teaspoon pepper
Angel hair pasta, cooked & hot
Freshly grated Parmesan cheese

Cook first 4 ingredients in olive oil over medium-high heat, stirring constantly, until tender. Add tomatoes and next seven ingredients, bring to a boil. Reduce heat, and simmer 30 minutes, stirring occasionally.

Serve over pasta, and sprinkle with Parmesan cheese. Garnish if desired. Yields 6 servings.

Myrtle Ann Saxon

Meat Balls and Tomato Sauce

We have enjoyed many wonderful "real Italian" meals with Gabe and Joe Ann DeGregorio. Joe Ann learned to cook from Gabe's mother who came from the old country—Italy. The following recipe includes many surprises and secrets of the Italian kitchen.

Tomato Sauce:
1-2 pounds chuck roast
28 ounces water
3 cans *(28 ounces)* Progresso tomatoes, blended in processor
3 cans *(28 ounces)* tomato puree
1 tablespoon fresh or dried basil
2 tablespoons salt (or to taste)
3 tablespoons sugar
¼ cup olive oil
2 medium onions, finely minced
4 cloves garlic
2 tablespoons Tony Chachere's seasoning (or to taste)

Pour olive oil in large pot (8 quarts). Saute onion and garlic, remove and set aside. Brown chuck roast on both sides. Then add blended tomatoes and puree with 28 ounces water and all the other seasonings. Bring to boil, then let simmer 2½ hours, stirring occasionally. While sauce is cooking, make meat balls.

Meat Balls:
1 pound ground chuck
2 cups stale Italian bread, soak in water then squeeze (not too dry)
4 cloves garlic, minced
3 eggs, well beaten
½ cup Romano cheese, grated
2 tablespoons fresh parsley, chopped
2 teaspoons salt
2 teaspoons pepper

Meat Balls (cont'd)

Mix eggs, bread, cheese, parsley, garlic, salt and pepper then add to ground beef and mix thoroughly. Wet hands to form meat balls, shape balls and place in pan to bake at 350 degrees for 20-30 minutes. Add meat balls to sauce when done and cook 30 minutes more. This recipe should make 24 meat balls and enough sauce for 2½ pounds spaghetti. Should feed 12-16 people.

Joe Ann De Gregorio

Miss Sis' Meat Balls

3 pounds ground beef
4 cloves garlic, minced
3 medium onions, minced
2 large eggs, whipped
1 large bell pepper, minced
4 cups bread crumbs
1 cup Parmesan or Romano grated cheese

Mix the above ingredients thoroughly, shape into small balls. Bake in 400-degree oven until brown or heat vegetable oil in skillet and brown evenly, turning several times.

These are genuine Italian meat balls to use with St. Joseph's Tomato Gravy (in this book) and spaghetti.

Miss Sis Runfalo

Eggs Sardou

2 cans artichokes
¼ cup green onions, chopped
½ cup butter
2 cups spinach, cooked and chopped
½ pint sour cream
1 tablespoon lemon juice
Salt and Pepper
Lea & Perrins Worcestershire sauce
4 eggs

Line up artichokes on cookie sheet, warm in oven. Sautee onions and butter. After few minutes, add spinach then sour cream, lemon juice and salt, pepper, Worcestershire to taste. Heat, but don't bake, mixture. Mound on each artichoke. Keep warm while you poach eggs. Put one poached egg on each artichoke. Cover with hollandaise (*see recipe on page 47 in this book*).

Maureen O'Keefe Ward

Garlic-Cheese Grits

1 16-ounce box yellow grits
6 cloves garlic, crushed
2 eggs, beaten
2½ sticks butter or Promise
16 ounces hot Mexican Velveeta cheese, cut up
3 hot banana peppers, finely minced
Mild Cheddar cheese, shredded
Salt to taste

Cook grits as directed on box. Add remaining ingredients, adding eggs gradually and stir thoroughly. Pour into large casserole and spread with mild shredded Cheddar cheese. Bake 30-40 minutes at 350 degrees. Remove from oven, let stand 5 minutes before serving as it will be very, very hot to touch.

Deedy Munro

Garlic-Cheese Grits (continued)

This recipe has been a long time favorite for holidays and special occasions. It was given to me by my friend Deedy Munro, famous in her own right for her dress shop specializing in formals and bridal wear, located in Ocean Springs, Mississippi. Her gowns have graced many Governor's Balls and Mardi Gras festivities and customers come from New Orleans, Mobile and Jackson, Mississippi. Deedy is also a marvelous cook.

Rose Annette O'Keefe

French Toast, 'Pain Perdu' or Lost Bread

6-8 slices stale bread, French or plain

4 eggs	1 stick margarine
2 tablespoons sugar	1 teaspoon vanilla
Powdered sugar or maple syrup	1 tablespoon cinnamon

Put one stick margarine in large skillet, melt over medium heat. Beat eggs, add sugar and milk with cinnamon and vanilla. Dip bread in mixture, lay in skillet to brown on both sides. Add more margarine if necessary. Serve with syrup or powdered sugar.

These are three names given to the same delicious breakfast treat.

Rose Annette O'Keefe

French Toast a la Pittsburgh

6 slices stale bread	1 stick butter or margarine
2 eggs	1 cup cornflakes
½ cup milk	½ teaspoon nutmeg

Beat together eggs, milk, and nutmeg. Dip bread in batter, then dip in cornflakes, fry in butter or margarine over medium heat.

Sam Ward

Blue Crab Omelet

½ pound crabmeat
6 eggs
½ cup mushrooms, chopped
½ cup onions, chopped
1 large bell pepper, diced

4-5 cloves garlic, minced
Pepper
Oregano
Paprika
Salt

Saute the onions in a frying pan with olive oil until they are very brown. This makes them sweet. When the onions are almost done, add the garlic and bell pepper, and brown slightly. Add the chopped mushrooms after the vegetables are almost done, then turn the stove on a low heat.

Beat all the eggs in a bowl, and when they are mixed thoroughly, add crabmeat, stir lightly, and then pour this mixture in the pan. Sprinkle salt, pepper, paprika and oregano over the top of the mixture. Then cover to cook for the duration. If you're in a Cajun mood, substitute red pepper for paprika.

This is a large omelet. It will feed four people, if you add some toast with it. Because of its size, it is better to let it cook slowly without attempting to flip it. Keep the lid cover over the pan while it is cooking.

This is John's favorite breakfast. Ooh la la!

John Michael O'Keefe, Sr.

DESSERTS

Susan O'Keefe Snyder, John O'Keefe, Joe O'Keefe and Virginia O'Keefe Brown (c. 1989) standing outside Baricev's restaurant on the waterfront in Biloxi, Mississippi. Baricev's was one of the top restaurants on the Coast for years, known especially for its great gumbo and seafood dishes. It has subsequently been replaced by the Biloxi Belle Steamer.

Kentucky Butter Cake

1½ cups butter
3 cups sugar
4 eggs
1 cup buttermilk
2 teaspoons vanilla

3 cups sifted flour
1 teaspoon baking powder
1 teaspoon salt
1 teaspoon soda
¼ cup water

In a bowl, cream 1 cup butter, gradually adding 2 cups sugar. Blend in 4 eggs, one at a time. In a separate bowl, combine 1 cup buttermilk and 2 teaspoons vanilla. Mix dry ingredients, flour, baking powder, salt and soda in a third bowl.

Add buttermilk and flour mixture to the butter and sugar, beginning with the flour mixture and alternating with the buttermilk. End with flour mixture. Grease and flour tube pan. Bake at 325 degrees for 60-65 minutes.

Topping:
Combine 1 cup sugar, ¼ cup water and ½ cup butter. Heat and pour over top of cake. Before pouring topping, take a fork and prick holes in the top of the cake so that the topping will seep through.

There is an interesting story behind this cake. The recipe originally came from Maureen O'Keefe when she was in the convent in St. Louis. Since then, it has been readily adopted as one of our favorite family recipes. Jeff and Justin O'Keefe have used this recipe many times with great success.

Anyway, to get back to the story. In the August of 1969 we (O'Keefe girls) had heard the radio and television reports that a ferocious hurricane—Hurricane Camille—was coming to the Gulf Coast, so I decided that I wanted to bake a Kentucky Butter Cake. Moma got very put-out with Dad and his daughters because we would not evacuate the house.

Kentucky Butter Cake (continued)

Finally, when the winds began to whip and the water started rising, a neighbor came to the house and told Moma that the water was covering all of Highway 90 and that they had been trying to evacuate their house and gotten flooded out. Moma told us that we could be foolish and stay for the cake, but she was leaving. After a while, when the cake was about half-cooked, Dad surveyed the highway situation and decided we should leave if we intended to get out by car. So we had to take the infamous cake out of the oven and, of course, it fell. However, we did get to eat it at Nannaw's house while we waited for the storm to blow over. Within the next 12 hours the entire first floor of our house was destroyed—including the kitchen.

Virginia O'Keefe Brown

One, Two, Three, Four Cake

½ pound butter or oleo
2 cups sugar
4 eggs
3 cups flour

1 cup milk
3 teaspoons baking powder
1 teaspoon vanilla

Cream butter and sugar; then add eggs. Sift flour and add alternately with milk and other ingredients. Add baking powder and vanilla at the last. For loaf pan, bake at 350 degrees for about 45 minutes; for cupcakes and layer cake bake at 375 degrees for about 15 or 20 minutes. Yield: 3 dozen cupcakes or 1 large cake of four layers.

Mrs. Teresa O'Keefe

I wish I had a nickel for every cake or batch of cupcakes Moma Tess cooked. She always referred to her cupcakes as "cookies."

Rose Annette O'Keefe

Italian Cream Cake

1 teaspoon of baking soda
1 cup buttermilk
5 eggs (separated)
2 cups of sugar
1 stick margarine

½ cup shortening
2 cups sifted, all-purpose flour
1 teaspoon vanilla
1 cup chopped pecans
1 cup of shredded coconut

Combine soda and buttermilk. Let stand until needed. Beat egg whites until stiff. Cream sugar, margarine and shortening. Add egg yolks, one at a time. Beat well after each addition. Add buttermilk and flour alternately, to cream mixture. Add vanilla. Fold in beaten egg whites, pecans and coconut. Bake in three 9-inch pans or four smaller pans, greased and floured at 325 degrees for 35 to 40 minutes.

Cream cheese frosting:
1 8-ounce package of cream cheese
1 stick margarine, softened
1 package powdered sugar
1 teaspoon vanilla

Mix ingredients thoroughly. Spread frosting between layers and on outside of cake. Sprinkle with pecans.

Virginia O'Keefe Brown

Pound Cake

8 eggs, separated
6 tablespoons sugar
1 pound butter
2¾ cups sugar

3½ cups flour
½ cup evaporated milk
1 tablespoon vanilla

Separate eggs and beat whites stiff with 6 tablespoons of sugar. Place in refrigerator. Cream butter and sugar, add egg yolks. Alternate flour and milk. Add vanilla. Fold in stiffly beat egg whites. Grease and flour large tube pan. Bake at 325 degrees for about 1½ hours.

Corita Johnson

Aunt Nell's Pecan-Raisin Cake

½ pound butter
1 cup sugar
8 eggs
¾ cup dark corn syrup
¾ cup whiskey, coffee or milk
2 boxes seedless raisins

1 level teaspoon soda
3 teaspoons baking powder
1 or 2 teaspoons cinnamon
4 cups pecans
3 cups flour

Cream butter, sugar and eggs. Add other ingredients. Grease and flour large tube pan. Bake in oven at 350 degrees for 1 hour and 15 minutes.

Teresa Slattery O'Keefe and Nell Slattery Tierney

Aunt Nell always made this cake for her Christmas gift. It's very good and not too rich.

Rose Annette O'Keefe

Miniature Cheese Cakes

24 vanilla wafers
3 8-ounce packages cream cheese
1 cup sugar
1 teaspoon vanilla
3 eggs
¼ teaspoon nutmeg
1 large can of fruit topping

Line 24 muffin tins with paper cups and place one vanilla wafer in the bottom of each cup. Blend cream cheese, sugar, vanilla, eggs and nutmeg. Then fill each cup two-thirds full of mixture.

Bake in preheated oven at 325 degrees for 20 -25 minutes or until set. Top with fruit topping of your choice. Yield: 24 miniature cakes.

Susan O'Keefe Snyder

Chocolate Sheet Fudge Cake

2 cups flour
2 cups sugar
½ teaspoon salt
2 sticks butter
3 tablespoons cocoa

1 cup water
2 eggs
½ cup buttermilk
1 teaspoon soda
1 teaspoon vanilla

Mix flour, sugar and salt. Melt butter, cocoa and 1 cup water. Add mixture to dry ingredients. Mix eggs, buttermilk, soda and vanilla. Add two mixtures together. Grease and flour cooke sheet or 9½ x 11" pan. Pour batter in and cook at 350 degrees for 20 minutes.

Icing:
1 stick butter
6 tablespoons milk
1 cup chopped pecans

2 tablespoons cocoa
¾ powdered sugar

Combine ingredients in small pot, heat and stir until evenly mixed. Put icing on when cake is still warm.

Virginia O'Keefe Brown

Aunt Caro's Sour Cream Cake Frosting

5 egg yolks
1 cup sugar

1 cup sour cream
1 cup chopped nuts

Beat egg yolks. Add sugar and sour cream. Cook in double boiler, stirring constantly until very thick. Remove from heat. Add nuts and spread between layers and on top of cake of your choice (Carrot Cake, Chocolate Cake, etc.).

Carolyn B. Sasser

Angel Food Cake

1¾ cups of unbeaten egg whites
1 generous pinch of salt
1 rounded teaspoon cream of tartar
1½ cups sugar
1¾ cups cake flour
1 teaspoon vanilla flavoring
1 teaspoon almond extract

Put the egg whites in mixing bowl. Add salt. Turn mixers on and beat til egg whites begin to get foamy. Add cream of tartar and continue beating until the whites are stiff (make a peak). Remove mixers and do the rest by hand.

Fold in the sugar and flour which have been sifted together five or six times. Add flavoring. Put in ungreased tube pan and bake at 350 degrees until done (45-60 minutes). Invert pan and let cool completely before removing from pan.

Rosemary Slattery Davis

Pineapple Ice Box Cake

½ stick butter   2 medium boxes vanilla wafers, crushed
1 cup sugar   1 can crushed pineapple
1 egg   1 teaspoon vanilla
1 cup pecans

Cream butter, sugar and egg. Add pecans, vanilla wafers, pineapple and vanilla. Mix well and put in refrigerator. When served, top with a little whipped cream.

Jo Tierney

Nannaw's Devil's Food Cake

1 cup butter	1 level teaspoon baking powder
1¼ cups sugar	1 level teaspoon baking soda
2 eggs	1 cup milk
1¾ cups flour	1 teaspoon vanilla
¾ cup cocoa	

Cream butter and sugar. Add eggs and milk, mix well. Sift flour, cocoa, baking soda and baking powder. Mix dry ingredients to other mixture a little at a time, blending well in between. Add vanilla last. Grease and flour tube pan. Bake at 375 degrees for about 20-25 minutes. Cool and remove from pans.

White Boiled Icing:

2 cups sugar	½ teaspoon salt
1 cup water	1 teaspoon vanilla
2 egg whites	½ teaspoon cream of tartar
	(*or lemon juice*)

Stir sugar and water until sugar dissolves, then bring to a boil. Cover and cook for about 3 minutes. Then uncover and cook to 240 degrees, or until syrup spins a thin thread. Whip 2 egg whites with ½ teaspoon of salt. Then pour syrup in a thin stream, whipping eggs constantly. Finally, add vanilla and cream of tartar. Spread over cake.

Teresa Slattery O'Keefe

Dirt Cake

8 ounces cream cheese, softened
¼ cup butter, softened
1 cup confectioner's sugar
1 pound bag Oreo cookies
6 ounces instant Vanilla pudding
¾ cup milk
12 ounces Cool Whip

Cream together cheese, butter and sugar. Crush Oreo's in food processor. Mix pudding and milk. Add to cheese mixture and fold in Cool Whip. Layer in 8" clear acrylic flower pot beginning and ending with the crushed Oreos. Decorate with gummy worms and silk flowers.

Fun for kids!! No cooking required!!

Maureen's Special Tarts

3 ounces cream cheese
½ cup butter

1 cup sifted flour
⅔ cup broken pecans

Mix cream cheese, butter and flour. Shape into balls about the size of a walnut. Press balls into tart pans. Drop a small amount of pecans into tart shell.

Filling:
1 egg
1 teaspoon vanilla
1 dash salt

¾ cup brown sugar
1 tablespoon soft butter

Combine ingredients in pot, melt and stir until evenly mixed. Pour about a tablespoon of brown sugar mixture into tart pans on top of pecans. Yield: 2 dozen.

Maureen O'Keefe Ward

Christmas Date Nut Cake

1 cup boiling water
2 sticks butter, melted
1 pound whole dates
1½ teaspoon baking soda
2 cups sifted flour
2 cups sugar
1 pinch salt

1 teaspoon cinammon
1 teaspoon nutmeg
2 cups pecans
2 eggs beaten
1 teaspoon vanilla
½ cup bourbon or brandy

Pour boiling water over melted butter and dates, sprinkle with baking soda. Combine flour, sugar, salt and spices, add to first mixture. To this mixture add pecans, beaten eggs, vanilla and bourbon or brandy.

Pour into greased tube pan and bake 1 hour at 350 degrees (when a straw comes out clean it is done). Cool cake on a rack for 20-25 minutes. To store, wrap the cake in brandy or bourbon soaked linen, then in foil, or you may make a few fine skewer punctures in cake and pour over it very slowly, drop by drop, ¼ to ½ cup liquor.

Lorelei Stroble

Banana Cake

½ cup shortening
1½ cups sugar
2 eggs
3 ripe bananas mashed
1 teaspoon vanilla

2 cups flour
¼ teaspoon salt
1 teaspoon baking powder
1 teaspoon baking soda
¾ cup milk

Cream shortening and sugar. Add eggs. Cream again then add bananas and vanilla flavoring. Sift all dry ingredients and add alternately with milk. Pour into greased and floured tube pan. Bake at 350 degrees for 50-60 minutes.

Virginia O'Keefe Brown

Cranberry-Orange Muffins

1¾ cups all-purpose flour
⅓ cup sugar
1 teaspoon baking powder
½ teaspoon baking soda
½ teaspoon salt
¾ cup buttermilk
½ cup vegetable oil
1 egg
1 cup fresh or frozen, thawed cranberries, finely chopped
½ cup (4 ounces) glace diced orange peel, finely chopped.
½ cup finely chopped walnuts
3 tablespoons orange juice
¾ cup sugar

Combine flour, ¾ cup sugar, baking powder, soda and salt in mixing bowl. Stir in combined buttermilk, oil and egg, stirring just until combined (do not overmix).

Fold in cranberries, orange peel and walnuts. Spoon batter into greased muffin tins. Bake in preheated 375-degree oven until toothpick inserted in centers of muffins comes out clean, 12-15 minutes for mini muffins, 20-25 minutes for regular muffins, 25-30 minutes for jumbo muffins.

Mix orange juice, ⅓ cup sugar; brush generously over muffins. Return to oven for 5 minutes. Cool muffins in pans 5 minutes; remove from pan and cool on wire racks. Makes 3 dozen mini muffins, 1 dozen regular muffins or ½ dozen jumbo muffins.

Lorelei Stroble

Lorelei has been a special friend of mine for many years. She is a wiz in the kitchen. She has opened and supervised many restaurants, taught cooking and catered many events. She truly deserves a chef's bonnet and neckerchief.

Rose Annette O'Keefe

Apple Pie Cake

5 cups sliced apples
1 stick butter
2 cups flour
2 cups sugar
2 teaspoons baking soda
2 teaspoons cinnamon

1 cup chopped nuts (optional)
1 cup raisins (optional)
1 teaspoon salt
2 teaspoons vanilla
2 teaspoons nutmeg

Mix all ingredients together. Place in greased large baking pan or tube pan. Bake at 350 degrees for one hour. When cool, sprinkle with powdered sugar and serve with hard sauce.

Hard Sauce:
1 stick butter
3 cups powdered sugar
3 teaspoons vanilla or 3 teaspoon bourbon.

Combine in mixer until blended.

Alice O'Keefe Sebastian

Angel Food Cake Divine

2 cups marshmallows
1 cup good brandy
1 pint whipping cream
2 dozen cherries or strawberries
1 (store bought) angel food cake

Cut marshmallows into quarters. Soak in brandy, stirring occasionally. Whip cream until stiff, fold in marshmallows and spread on cake. Garnish with cherries or strawberries. This topping would go well on pound cake also.

Desserts have never been my forte, our daughters do the honors. This recipe is so easy and great, even I can do it! You'll like it too. Delicious!

Rose Annette O'Keefe

Carrot Cake

2 cups sugar
4 eggs
1 cup oil
2 ¼ cups flour
2 teaspoons baking soda

1 teaspoon vanilla
3 cups grated carrots
2 teaspoons cinnamon
2 teaspoons baking powder

Blend sugar and eggs. Add other ingredients and mix well. Bake in a greased and floured bundt pan or in three 8" cake pans at 350 degrees.

Cream cheese icing:
1 box powdered sugar
8 ounces cream cheese

2 tablespoons milk
1 stick butter

Virginia O'Keefe Brown

Butterpecan Crumble Crust

1 stick butter, softened
¼ cup brown sugar, packed
1 cup sifted flour
½ cup pecans, chopped

Mix above ingredients and spread in 9x13" baking pan. Bake at 400 degrees for 15 minutes. Remove from oven; stir and crumble the crust with a spoon. Use some of the crumb mixture to press in the bottom of a 9" pie pan (to be used for any type of icebox pie). Use remaining crumb crust as a sprinkle for the top of the pie.

Cecilia O'Keefe Neustrom

Upside-Down Apple Pie

½ stick butter, melted
1 cup brown sugar
1 cup pecan halves
2 pie crusts

2 cups sliced apples
2 teaspoons nutmeg
1 cup white & brown sugar mixed
Cinammon

Coat bottom and sides of pie pan with melted butter, spreading evenly. Then pack brown sugar on bottom and sides. Place pecan halves, flat side up, in design of your choice on bottom of pan in sugar. Lay one pie crust on top.

Cover with sliced apples, cinnamon, nutmeg and sugar. Place second pie crust on top. Put pie pan on cookie sheet to prevent overflow in oven. Bake at 350 degrees for one hour. When brown and done, put plate on top of pie plate and flip over—voila!

Alice Sebastian

Blackberry Cobbler

6 cups fresh blackberries
 (handpicked)

2 tablespoons cornstarch
1 cup sugar

Crust:
1½ cups flour
¾ cup sugar

¼ teaspoon salt
½ cup butter

Fill a baking dish with the blackberries. Mix cornstarch in with sugar and pour mixture over the blackberries. Sift together the flour, sugar and salt. Cut the butter into the flour mixture until it has a crumbly texture. Sprinkle over the berries and bake at 350 degrees for about 45 minutes, or until browned.

Kathryn O'Keefe

Chocolate Ice Box Pie

1 stick margarine
1 cup pecans
1 cup flour
8 ounces cream cheese
12 ounces Cool Whip
1 small box instant vanilla & chocolate pudding

1 cup powdered sugar
1 teaspoon vanilla
3 cups milk
1 grated chocolate candy bar

Mix margarine, ½ cup pecans and flour press flat in a 9 x 13 pan. Bake at 350 degrees for 20-25 minutes. Mix cream cheese, 4 ounces Cool Whip and sugar and spread on top of cooled crust mixture.

Mix instant pudding, milk and vanilla and carefully place on top of cream cheese layer. Spread 8 ounces of Cool Whip on top of pie. Spread grated chocolate on top and sprinkle with finely chopped pecans. Keep in refrigerator.

Pecan Pie

½ cup sugar
1 cup dark Karo syrup
4 tablespoons butter
3 eggs, beaten
1 teaspoon vanilla
1 cup pecans
1 uncooked pie shell

Cook sugar and syrup until sugar melts. Add butter and, when melted, add syrup mixture slowly to beaten eggs. Add vanilla and pecans, pour in unbaked pie shell. Bake at 450 degrees for ten minutes, then at 350 degress for 50 minutes. Yield: 1 large pie.   *Carolyn B. Sasser*

Aunt Caro was an artist in the kitchen and baked the prettiest pies. She excelled in cooking, fine crochet, quilting and smocking little girls' dresses. She liked to fish too and was a wonderful sport.
                                        Rose Annette O'Keefe

Chocolate Cream Pie

2 tablespoons Crisco (or oleo)   ¾ cup sugar
4 tablespoons flour   ¼ teaspoon salt
1 ½ cups milk   3 eggs (yolks only)
2 squares chocolate   1 teaspoon vanilla
1 baked pie shell

Meringue:
3 tablespoons sugar   3 egg whites

Melt oleo, add flour, milk and chocolate (cut in pieces), sugar, salt and bring slowly to boiling stirring until thick and smooth. It will look "curdly" then smooth. Remove from fire and add beaten eggs and vanilla. Pour in baked shell when cool. Add meringue of sugar and egg whites. Bake at 325 degrees until golden brown.

                                        Carolyn B. Sasser

French Apple Pie

2 cups flour	½ to ⅔ cups sugar
½ teaspoon salt	1 teaspoon cinnamon
⅓ cup lard	½ cup + 2 tablespoons butter
6-8 apples	½ cup brown sugar

Mix 1 cup flour, ½ teaspoon salt and ⅓ cup lard to make pastry. Line pan and chill thoroughly. Pare and core apples, slice thin. Mix sugar, cinnamon and 2 teaspoon flour with apples. Dot with 2 tablespoons butter.

Cream ½ cup butter and ½ cup brown sugar. Work in 1 cup flour. Sprinkle crumb mixture over top of apple mixture. Bake 35-45 minutes in a hot oven (400 degrees) for the first 15 minutes, then slow (300).

Carolyn B. Sasser

Pineapple Cake Pie

1 cup sugar	1 teaspoon grated lemon rind
3 tablespoons flour	½ cup canned pineapple
½ teaspoon salt	*(crushed and drained)*
3 eggs, separated	1 cup milk, heated
3 tablespoons lemon juice	

Mix sugar, flour and salt. Add egg yolks, beaten light, with lemon juice. Mix well. Add rind and pineapple. Stir in milk. Fold in stiffly beaten egg whites. Line fairly deep pie pan with unbaked crust. Brush with melted Crisco. Pour in filling. Bake in quick oven (400 degrees) for 10 minutes. Lower heat to moderate (350 degree) oven. Bake 35-45 minutes more. Chill.

Carolyn B. Sasser

Peaches & Cream (Kinda Like Cobbler)

1 stick butter	1 large can sliced peaches
¾ cup flour	½ cup sugar
1 large box vanilla pudding mix	¾ cup peach juice
2 tablespoons baking powder	8 ounces cream cheese

Melt butter. Add flour, dry pudding, and baking powder. Spoon into medium sized casserole dish. Mash with spoon to cover the bottom of the dish (it will be a thin layer).

Drain the peaches. Save the juice in a bowl. Pour the peaches over crust mixture. Mix well sugar, ¾ cup peach juice and cream cheese. Pour over peaches. Sprinkle cinnamon on top. Bake at 350 degrees for 30-45 minutes.

Mercedes O'Keefe Huval

Chocolate Pie

1 ⅓ cups sugar
2 level tablespoons flour
3 egg yolks, beaten
⅓ cup cocoa
⅔ cup boiling water
¾ stick butter or margarine, melted

Mix sugar and flour. Mix cocoa and boiling water until smooth. Add to sugar mixture. Add egg yolks and butter. Blend well. Pour into unbaked pie shell and bake at 350 degrees until firm. Top with meringue. Serve in small slices— very rich.

Patricia Victoria O'Keefe

Buttermilk Chess Pie

2 cups sugar
2 tablespoons all-purpose flour
5 large eggs
⅔ cup buttermilk
4 tablespoons butter or margarine, melted
1 teaspoon vanilla extract
1 unbaked 9-inch pastry shell

Combine sugar and flour in a large bowl: add eggs and buttermilk, stirring until blended. Stir in butter (if butter is hot, pour in slowly, better is lukewarm) and vanilla and pour into unbaked pastry shell. Bake at 350 degrees for 45 minutes or until set. Check for doneness after minimum baking time by gently shaking the pie. The center should be set with a slight jiggle. Cool on a wire rack. Optional: Sprink 3 tablespoons corn meal over top before baking to create crust.

Myrtle Ann Saxon

Peanut Butter Cookies

1 cup brown sugar
1 cup white sugar
1 cup shortening
1 cup peanut butter
1 egg

1 teaspoon vanilla
1 teaspoon salt
2 teaspoons baking soda
3 cups flour

Cream sugar and shortening. Add eggs, peanut butter, flour, soda, salt and vanilla. Roll into balls. Pat on cookie sheet with fork. Bake for 15 minutes in 375 degree oven.

Carolyn B. Sasser

Honey Cookies

½ cup shortening
½ cup sugar
⅓ cup honey
1 egg

½ teaspoon salt
1 teaspoon baking powder
2 cups flour
1 ½ teaspoons vanilla

Cream honey, shortening and sugar. Add egg, vanilla and dry ingredients. Chill. Cut in slices. Place on greased cookie sheet and bake at 375 degree oven for 8-10 minutes.

Carolyn B. Sasser

Cream Cheese Cookies

¼ cup shortening
3 packages cream cheese
⅔ cup sugar
¼ teaspoon baking powder

¼ teaspoon salt
1½ cups flour
1 teaspoon almond extract

Cream shortening, cheese and sugar. Add almond extract and dry ingredients. Shape dough into roll and chill. Slice and place on greased cookie sheet. Bake at 375-degree oven for 8-10 minutes.

Carolyn B. Sasser

Oatmeal Goodies

1½ cups shortening
2 cups brown sugar
3 eggs
2 cups rolled oats
1 cup chopped pecans
Sugar to roll them in

1 pinch salt
2 teaspoons soda
1 teaspoon cinnamon
3¾ cups flour
1 cup raisins

Cream shortening and sugar together. Add eggs, oatmeal, pecans and raisins. Add flour, cinnamon, soda and salt. Roll into small balls. Dip in sugar. Press down with bottom of a glass covered with a cloth. Makes 10 dozen. Place on greased cookie sheet and bake in 375 degree oven until golden.

Carolyn B. Sasser

Rolled Oatmeal Cookies

1 cup shortening
1 cup white sugar
1 teaspoon vanilla
1 teaspoon baking soda
½ cup of nuts, finely chopped

1 cup brown sugar
2 eggs, beaten
1 ½ cups flour
3 cups oatmeal

Mix together in following order: shortening, brown sugar, white sugar, eggs, vanilla, flour, baking soda, oatmeal, and nuts. Shape dough into 4 rolls. Wrap each roll in wax paper and chill for at least 2 hours. Slice and bake on ungreased cookie sheet at 350 degrees.

Virginia O'Keefe Brown

Peanut Butter Cookies

1 cup shortening

1 cup brown sugar

1 teaspoon vanilla

2 cups flour

½ teaspoon salt

1 cup sugar

2 eggs

1 cup peanut butter

2 teaspoons baking soda

Mix ingredients, bake cookies at 350 degrees for 10 minutes.

Virginia O'Keefe Brown

Virginia has always loved to bake and does so in great volume. Her cookies are always a big hit with the kids—and everyone else.

Moma Ceci's Ice Box Cookies

1½ cups butter or oleo

1⅓ cups white sugar

⅔ cup brown sugar

3 beaten eggs

1 cup nuts

5 cups flour

1 teaspoon soda

1 teaspoon salt

Cream butter and sugar, add eggs, then dry ingredients. Shape in 1½ inch roll and refrigerate over night. Slice thin and bake on ungreased cookie sheet at 375 degrees until light brown.

Cecile B. Saxon

Ceci always made these wonderful cookies for her Christmas boxes. It is impossible to eat only one, they are so yum-yum good.

Rose Annette O'Keefe

Pecan Fingers

1 cup butter or oleo
⅓ cup sugar
2 teaspoons vanilla
2 teaspoons water

Powdered sugar
1 cup chopped pecans
2 cups sifted flour

Cream butter and sugar. Add vanilla and water. Add flour and pecans. Chill for 3-4 hours. Shape into fingers. Bake on ungreased cookie sheet at 325 degrees for 20 minutes or until brown.
Roll in powdered sugar while still warm.

Virginia O'Keefe Brown

Chewy Date Bars

1 cup brown sugar, firmly packed
¾ cup flour
1 pinch salt
1 teaspoon baking powder
1 ½ cups dates
1 ½ cups chopped pecans
2 beaten eggs
1 teaspoon vanilla
½ cup powdered sugar

Mix sugar, flour, baking powder and salt. Then add dates, nuts, eggs and vanilla. Spread mixture in greased 9x12" baking pan and bake at 300 degrees for 25 minutes. When done, cut in bars and sprinkle with powdered sugar.

Aunt Edna

Aunt Edna loved to cook and sew, and she had a marvelous sense of humor. She used to be a milliner of fine ladies' hats, or chapeaux.

Rose Annette O'Keefe

Butterscotch Brownies

1 pound light or dark brown sugar
2 cups flour
2½ teaspoons baking powder
2 sticks of butter or oleo
2 cups chopped pecans/walnuts
2 eggs
1 teaspoon vanilla

Melt butter and brown sugar over low heat. Remove and let cool. Add eggs one at a time, stirring well after each. Add vanilla. Then add the flour and pecans and finally the baking powder.

Bake in 8 x 11 inch pain (or so) for 25 minutes (or so) at 350 degrees. Let cool, then cut, then enjoy!!

Susan Davis Flanagan

Toffee Bars

1 package Keebler Honey Graham crackers (not box)
1 stick butter   1 stick oleo
½ cup sugar   1 cup chopped pecans

Break graham crackers into squares and put onto greased cookie sheet. Pre-heat oven to 350 degrees. Bring butter and oleo to a boil, add sugar and cook for 2 minutes. Spoon mixture over crackers. Sprinkle pecans liberally. Bake for 10 minutes. Let cool in tray for a few minutes, then remove.

Virginia O'Keefe Brown

Aunt Caro's Scones

2 cups flour
3 teaspoons baking powder
½ teaspoon salt
2+ tablespoons sugar

Milk
2 eggs
¼ cup fat or shortening

Sift together flour, baking powder, salt, 2 tablespoons sugar. Cut in fat. Beat eggs, add with milk to make soft dough. Knead lightly. Roll ½ inch thick. Brush with milk and sprinkle with sugar. Cut in squares, fold over and cook in hot oven (425 degrees) for 15 minutes.

Carolyn B. Sasser

Mary Mahoney's Pusharattas

5 pounds self-rising flour
½ cup sugar
6 orange peelings, grated
3 whole apples, grated
6 lemon peelings, grated

3 cups raisins
½ cup whiskey
3 tablespoons vanilla
½ gallon milk
2 cups pecans, grated

Mix flour and sugar together first. Then combine grated pecans, apples, oranges, lemons and raisins (not grated) together. Empty these ingredients into the flour and sugar and mix well together. Add milk, whiskey and vanilla to the ingredients. Mix well together. In teaspoon-full lumps, deep fat fry pusharata batter until golden brown.

Glaze:
6 boxes confectioner's sugar
½ teaspoon almond extract
4 cans evaporated milk

Mix confectioner's sugar, almond extract and Pet milk. Glaze pusharatas while they are still hot from frying. Yield: About 300 pusharatas.

Mary Mahoney

Mrs. Savarro's Pralines

1½ cups light brown sugar
1½ cups white (granulated) sugar
3 tablespoons dark Karo corn syrup
1 cup evaporated milk

1½ cups pecans
2 tablespoons butter
1 teaspoon vanilla
1 pinch salt

Mix together light brown sugar, white sugar, Karo syrup, milk and pinch salt. Boil until mixture reaches a soft ball—drop about ½ teaspoon into a cup of cold water. When you're able to do this and pick up the dropping and make a soft ball, it's ready to take off the heat.

Remove from heat and add vanilla, butter and pecans. Stir until butter melts. Let mixture cool a few minutes and then beat until mixture begins to lose its gloss and thicken. Quickly drop tablespoons of mixture onto wax paper or buttered foil. Let cool until they're able to be lifted from paper.   *Kathryn O'Keefe*

Mrs. Savarro had a small neighborhood grocery store near our home. She is a wonderful friend who has always been kind to our kids and a good influence too.

Rose Annette O'Keefe

Aunt Caro's Pralines

3 cups white sugar
3 tablespoons butter
3 cups of pecans

1 cup evaporated milk
¼ teaspoon of salt
2 teaspoons of vanilla

Put two cups of sugar, cream butter and salt in a large, heavy pot. Bring to boil, stirring, then continue cooking over low heat. Put other cup of sugar in small, heavy skillet over medium heat and stir until caramelized. Stir slowly in first mixture, cook to soft ball stage (which only takes a few minutes). Allow to cool, then beat until mixture thickens. Then spoon quickly onto wax paper to finish hardening.

Carolyn B. Sasser

Moma Ceci's Caramels

2 cups of sugar
1 stick butter
One pinch salt
4-6 cups chopped pecans

1½ cups of dark Karo syrup
2 cups evaporated milk
2 teaspoons vanilla

Mix sugar, butter, Karo, salt and 1 cup of evaporated milk. Boil a few minutes. Add other cup of Pet cream. Stir constantly and cook just below 50 degrees on candy thermometer until firm ball stage. Add vanilla and pecans, pour into greased 12x12 pan. When cold, cut in squares and wrap in wax paper.

Cecile B. Saxon

Ceci was master of the art, but Justin O'Keefe followed in her footsteps.   *Rose Annette O'Keefe*

Divinity

2½ cups sugar
½ cup water
Pinch of salt

½ cup white Karo syrup
2 egg whites

Boil sugar, water, Karo until it forms a long thread hanging from spoon. Pour into bowl of stiffly beaten egg whites. Beat til it hardens enough to drop from spoon. Add nuts by hand. Drop on handi-wrap.

Jo Tierney

Jeremiah Joseph O'Keefe Sr. (c. 1944) in the cockpit of a U.S. Marine Corsair fighter plane. His officers gave him a half-day pass to get married to Rose Annette Saxon. On early morning training flights during his honeymoon, he would swoop down in his plane and buzz their apartment to wake Annette up.

Dec. 20, 1944
Wed. Morning

Good morning sweetheart,
      That was a mighty small letter I wrote last night honey but I was tired out and had an early rise this morning. This morning I'm taking off to do some letter writing . . . .
      The day before yesterday I got three packages and they really look inviting. The one from you had the catsup and the sauce in it and I've already gotten crabmeat from Momma so I am all set. The box from Momma Ces was filled with wonderful pralines and caramels and I am trying hard to hold them until Christmas. The other box was from Nicki and had a "Don't open until Christmas" on it, so I'm saving that one. So far all the boxes have gotten here in

Affection and Confections . . .

fine shape except the first one from Momma. Please thank Moma
Ces for me and I intend to get a letter off to her this afternoon.

. . . Honey I wish I could be there to pace the floor and
sweat it out with you. I'll probably be doing it out here anyway. I
can hardly wait to find out the news but suppose I'll just have to be
patient and wait.

Dearest, I love you so much and do pray that you have the
baby easily. That is about the only thing I could think of these days.
I'll close for now honey but will be with you again tomorrow. Good
night little angel.

I love you so much,

_____

My dearest wife,

Today was another red letter day and I got two sweet letters
from you and one from Momma. This afternoon some boat mail
came in and guess which package I got first! — the box of books.
My mouth was watering and when I opened it up and saw the
books, well, you can imagine I was a little disappointed. Honey
don't think I don't appreciate them though, because I have looked
them over and know I will enjoy them. Thanks a lot sweetheart. I
have one other registered package which I'll get this afternoon and
I'm anxious to find out what is in it . . .

I guess Jerry Jr. is just getting anxious to see what the
world looks like and that is why he's getting so rambunctious these
days. You must be getting anxious yourself darling and I can
understand it because your ol' man is anxious too . . .

I love you so much,
Jerry

Heavenly Hash

50 large marshmallows
3 large Hershey bars with almonds or one bar of cocoa butter nuts (optional)

Quarter marshmallows. Melt Hershey bars. Blend in marshmallows and extra nuts. Refrigerate until hard. Cut into squares and serve.

Cecilia O'Keefe Neustrom

Katie Carron's Pepper Jelly

6 ounces Certo (1 box, both pouches)
6 cups sugar
1½ cups cider vinegar
¾ cup chopped green peppers
¼ cup chopped red peppers

Combine sugar, vinegar, red and green peppers. Cook to hard boil, careful not to over stir. Remove from heat, let stand for five minutes. Add Certo, pour into jars, then seal. One bar of melted Gulf wax is usually enough per batch.

Susan Carron

Swedish Spritz

1½ cups butter, softened
1 cup sugar
1 well-beaten egg, room temperature
1 teaspoon vanilla
1 teaspoon almond flavoring
4 cups sifted white flour
1 teaspoon baking powder

Mix in order listed. Force through cookie press. Decorate with colored sugar or jam. Bake at 400 degrees for 8 to 10 minutes. Note: cookie dough is easiest to use when kept cool.

Cecilia O'Keefe Neustrom

Mrs. Teresa O'Keefe, known affectionately as "Nannaw," for years hosted a big Sunday dinner of fried chicken for her children and grandchildren; the tradition was later transferred to the home of her son Jerry and his wife, Rose Annette. Nannaw is shown here, at the age of 97, with Dr. John O'Keefe (c. 1992).

Rustulas

3 eggs	3 tablespoons sugar
1 teaspoon vanilla	2 cups flour
¼ teaspoon salt	Confectioner's sugar
2 tablespoons melted butter	

Beat eggs. Add sugar, salt, butter and vanilla. Mix until blended. Add flour to make dough smooth. Knead until well blended and elastic. Wrap in waxed paper, place in bowl, cover with towel and put in warm place for 1 hour. Then take part of dough and roll out as thin as possible. Cut into strips and tie into a knot. Fry dough in very hot deep oil until browned lightly. Remove and sprinkle with confectioner's sugar.

Lucy Mavar

Peanut Butter & Jelly

This is a kid's first recipe.

Ingredients:
Bread
Peanut Butter
Jelly

Take two slices of bread put them on top of the table. Unscrew the top from the jars of peanut butter and jelly.

Take one large butter knife and dig out a big glob of peanut butter and spread it on one of the pieces of bread. Spread it real hard so that the inside of the bread breaks a little bit and curls up toward the knife. Then push the curled-up piece back down with your fingers, and lick them afterward. Plus, take one or two licks off of the knife full of peanut butter.

Use the same knife, with peanut butter still on it, to dig into the jar of jelly (grape is preferable because the peanut butter stains show up better), and get a bunch of the grape jelly out to spread on the other piece of bread. Leave lots of traces of peanut butter in the jelly jar. This will gross other people out and leave more for you, later. Or you can reverse the order and do the jelly first. Either way, leave a good trail.

Try to put the jelly top on the peanut butter jar, and the peanut butter top on the jelly jar, and when you find you can't do it, then leave both tops off, remembering how hungry you are.

Smash down the two pieces of bread together, so that some of the mixture spills out, and then lick off the rest. Hold tightly to the sandwich right near where you are biting into it. This will let the back part of the sandwich fall open, so that some of the insides can spill onto the floor for the house animals.
Pour a big glass of milk to the very top of the glass, and maybe a little extra just to make sure, then drink it down, spilling a little.

Peanut Butter & Jelly (cont'd)

This will give you a nice big white mustache to go with the purple and brown one you already have from the sandwich.

Leave the half-full glass of milk on the table and go outside to finish your sandwich, where it's more fun to eat. Finish half or one-third of it, then throw the rest in the dirt for the outside animals, and continue playing.

Come back inside in one half-hour to 45 minutes and tell your Mom that you're hungry.

John Michael O'Keefe

Grape Juice Lemon Punch

1 large bottle Welch's Grape Juice	2 tablespoons sugar
3 lemons, juice of	1 quart water

Put above in large pitcher, combine well, serve over ice. Very refreshing.

To discourage our children from soda pops when they were small, we served this punch often. We all liked it.

Rose Annette O'Keefe

Cranberry Cocktail

1 pound cranberries	Juice of one lemon
1 quart plus 2 cups water	1 or 2 cups orange juice
1 cup sugar	2 cups water

Simmer cranberries in 1 quart water until done. Strain. Boil sugar and 2 cups water until sugar is melted. Add to cranberry juice. Add orange juice and lemon juice just before serving.

Carolyn B. Sasser

Little and Lively Fruit Tart

1 16-ounce Angel food cake
4 tablespoons peach preserves
4 cups frozen low fat vanilla yogurt
½ cup blueberries
2 peaches or nectarines
1 kiwi fruit
6-8 strawberries

Angel food cake may be purchased from bakery or use your favorite recipe. Split angel food cake in half, horizontally, fit into a 9 inch pie plate. Fill in hole with part of second half. Spoon frozen yogurt on top of cake. Place in freezer, covered with plastic wrap. Peel and slice peaches, wash and slice strawberries, wash and drain blueberries, peel and slice kiwi. Refrigerate in separate containers. About 45 minutes before serving time, arrange fruit over yogurt. Ring outer edge with peaches, second layer with strawberries, next layer with kiwi and fill in center with blueberries. Put peach preserves in microwave for 30 seconds and pour over fruit to glaze. Return to freezer for 30 minutes or less. Slice in wedges and serve. May garnish with a sprig of mint. Fruit of your choice may be substituted for the above selection. Preparation time 30 minutes. Serves 8.

Lorelei Stroble

Ceci's Peanut Butter Fudge

3 cups sugar
1 can evaporated milk
1 ½ sticks butter

1 teaspoon vanilla
1 7-ounce jar marshmallow cream
1 cup peanut butter

Combine sugar, evaporated milk and butter. Cook to soft ball stage. Then stir in peanut butter, marshmallow cream and vanilla. Pour into 9" x 13" buttered pan.

Cecilia O'Keefe Neustrom

Katie's Bourbon Balls

2½ boxes powdered sugar
¾ cup bourbon
½ bar Gulf wax paraffin
1 stick and 2 tablespoons butter
1 cup finely chopped pecans
2 boxes Baker's semi-sweet chocolate

Mix sugar, butter, bourbon and nuts in food processor. Then put in refrigerator or freezer covered. When ready, make small balls and put back in cooler. Melt chocolate and wax in double boiler. Dip balls in and out, put on wax paper until firm. Makes 100 balls.

Susan Carron

Peanut Butter Fudge

2 cups sugar
2 tablespoons Karo syrup (light)
⅔ cup pet milk
⅓ cup whole milk

3 tablespoons peanut butter
1 teaspoon vanilla
1 tablespoon butter
1 dash salt

Combine sugar, syrup, milks and salt. Boil on high until mixture reaches soft ball stage. Remove from heat and add butter, vanilla and peanut butter. Beat mixture until it thickens enough to pour into a buttered 8" square cake pan. *To make it extra good—melt chocolate and pour on top of peanut butter fudge.

Virginia O'Keefe Brown

Caramel Peanut Butter Squares

2 eggs
½ cup peanut butter
1 ¼ cups brown sugar

½ cup chopped nuts
½ teaspoon salt
½ cup flour

Beat eggs until light. Stir in peanut butter, then butter, then brown sugar. Mix well. Add dry ingredients. Pour into greased pan. Bake for 25 minutes in slow oven.

Carolyn B. Sasser

Mary Mahoney's Bread Pudding

6 slices day old bread
2 cups milk
2 tablespoons plus ½ cup sugar
2 tablespoons melted butter

1 teaspoon cinnamon
4 eggs
½ cup seedless raisins
1 teaspoon vanilla extract

Break bread in small pieces in baking dish (about 1 ½-quart size). Sprinkle cinnamon over bread and add raisins and melted butter. Toast lightly bread mixture in oven at about 350 degrees. Then add mixture of eggs, sugar, milk and vanilla extract, after mixing well. Bake about 30 minutes or until solid. Traditionally served with rum sauce. Serves about 8.

Mary Mahoney

Cecilia's Bread Pudding

3 large eggs
¾ cup sugar
1 teaspoon vanilla
1 cup regular milk
1 cup evaporated milk

¾ stick butter, melted
½ teaspoon salt
3-4 slices buttered toast
Nutmeg (optional)

Whip eggs and add sugar, vanilla, milk, butter and salt. Pour in 8 x 8" pan. Slice toast in small pieces and place on top of mixture and dunk them to moisten the tops. Sprinkle lightly with nutmeg. Place pan in a larger baking dish that has been filled with about 1 inch of water. Bake at 350 degrees for 35 minutes.   *Cecilia O'Keefe Neustrom, courtesy of Ann Lane*

Kat's Family Fudge

⅔ cup Hershey's cocoa
3 cups sugar
1/8 teaspoon salt
1 teaspoon vanilla

¼ cup butter or margarine
1½ cups pet milk
2 tablespoons dark Karo syrup

Thoroughly combine cocoa, sugar and salt in heavy 4-quart saucepan; stir in milk. Bring to rolling boil on medium heat, stirring constantly. boil without stirring to 234 degrees (soft-ball stage) or until a small amount of mixture dropped into cold water forms a soft ball which flattens on removal from water. (Bulb of candy thermometer should not rest on bottom of saucepan.)

Remove from heat; add butter or margarine and vanilla. Do Not Stir! Cool at room temperature to 110 degrees, beat until fudge thickens and loses some of its gloss. Quickly spread in lightly buttered 8- or 9-inch square pan; cool. Cut into squares. Makes 3 dozen squares.

Marshmallow-Nut Variation—Increase cocoa to ¾ cup , cook fudge as above. Add 1 cup marshmallow cream with butter or margarine and vanilla. Do Not Stir! Cool to 110 degrees. Beat 10 minutes; stir in 1 cup broken nuts and pour into pan. (Fudge does not set until poured into pan.)

Although this recipe is not an original "O'Keefe" recipe it should be included in our family collection of recipes because it was always a favorite — cooked and enjoyed by all of us, with our own variation added in later years.

Kathryn O'Keefe

Blintzes (Crepes)

1 cup milk	2 eggs
¼ cup flour	Salt and sugar to taste

Combine milk, eggs and flour to make batter. Pour a thin layer into greased frying pan. Cook until brown and flip to brown on other side. When crepes are done, add filling mixture to each one, roll and sprinkle with powdered sugar.

Filling:

Cottage cheese	Fruit
Sour cream	Sugar
Cinnamon	Raisins
1 cup powdered sugar	

Cecilia O'Keefe Neustrom
as given by Dina Landskroner, Jerusalem

Biskatina

3 tablespoons Crisco	1 teaspoon Anise essence
¾ cup butter	1 teaspoon cinnamon
2 cups sugar	1 teaspoon salt
4 eggs	1 tablespoon baking powder
3 tablespoons vinegar	2½ cups flour
1 tablespoon vanilla	2 cups pecans, chopped fine
3 tablespoons whiskey	

Preheat oven to 325-350 degrees. Cream Crisco, butter and sugar very well. Add eggs, one at a time. Then add vinegar, vanilla, whiskey, anise, cinnamon, salt and baking powder. Blend. Add flour gradually until you have soft dough that can be rolled. Add pecans last. Roll out dough to 1 and ½ inch thickness, then make a roll. Bake 20-25 minutes on greased sheet. Cut immediately into ¼-½ inch slices. Place on cookie sheet. Bake in top of oven at 450 degrees for 3-4 minutes. Cool, then store.

Lucy Mavar

Caramel Custard

½ cup white sugar   ¼ cup water
6 custard cups (4-5 ounces)

Combine sugar and water in a small saucepan and stir occasionally with a wooden spoon until dark brown. Pour into custard cups.

½ cup sugar   3 large eggs
⅛ teaspoon salt   2 large egg yolks
¼ teaspoon vanilla   2 cups milk

Blend sugar, eggs, egg yolks, salt and vanilla. Scald milk and mix into other ingredients. Place cups in baking pan with 1-1 ½ inches water. Bake in preheated oven at 325 degrees for 40 to 45 minutes, or until knife can be inserted and withdrawn clean. Place cups on cooling rack for ½ hour. Put in refrigerator.

Kathryn O'Keefe

Caramel Butter Pecan Ice Cream

2 cups chopped pecans
½ stick butter
2 cups sugar
4 cups heavy whipping cream
1 jar butterscotch caramel sauce
  (*Mrs. Richardson's*)

¼ teaspoon salt
2 tablespoons vanilla
4 cups milk
Rock salt
Crushed ice

Place chopped pecans and butter in small roasting pan and roast at 425 degrees for 15-20 minutes, stirring often. Let cool completely.

Combine whipping cream, sugar and vanilla in mixing bowl. Beat with mixer until stiff. Add salt and milk to cream mixture and blend well. Add cooled chopped pecans and mix well. Follow instructions on ice cream freezer. Be sure to use crushed ice as this forms a smoother ice cream.

When ice cream is finished churning add caramel sauce. Sauce can be added to freezer can by poking a long handled wooden spoon into mixture and filling holes or the entire mixture can be transferred to another container, layering sauce and ice cream. Place in freezer over night to fully harden. Makes 6 quarts.

I like this one the best and have had several proposals for marriage when making it.

Chris Snyder

Peach Custard Ice Cream

10 pounds peaches, peeled and sugared
2 quarts milk   2 cups sugar
2 teaspoons vanilla   6 eggs (small)

Scald milk. Add beaten eggs, sugar and vanilla. Let cool. Add peaches. Use 1 small carton whipping cream to top off the ice cream mixture in the freezer. Follow instructions on ice cream freezer. Be sure to use crushed ice as this forms a smoother ice cream. Makes 6 quarts.

Chris Snyder

Strawberry Ice Cream

1½ cups sugar   Crushed ice
4 cups heavy whipping cream   Rock salt
1 cup milk   ¼ teaspoon salt
4 cups sweetened   2 tablespoons vanilla
   fresh strawberries

Clean berries, cut in half and sprinkle with sugar. Refrigerate until needed. Combine whipping cream, sugar and vanilla in mixing bowl. Beat with mixer until stiff. Puree 2½ cups of berries until smooth. Chop remaining berries to size you prefer in ice cream. Add berries, salt and milk to cream mixture and blend well.

Follow instructions on ice cream freezer. Be sure to use crushed ice as this forms a smoother ice cream. Makes 6 quarts. Same basic recipe works for peaches or dewberries.

Chris Snyder

The Best Banana Nut Bread

1½ cup sugar   ½ cup shortening
2 eggs   ¼ teaspoon salt
1½ teaspoon baking soda   3 cups flour
¾ cups sour milk (1½ tablespoons vinegar plus milk)
3 mashed ripe bananas   ½ cup nuts

Blend sugar and shortening together. Add eggs, salt and baking soda dissolved in a bit of hot water. Add alternately flour and sour milk mixture. Stir in mashed bananas and nuts. Bake 45-60 minutes in a greased loaf pan at 350 degrees. Yield: 2 loaves.

Maureen O'Keefe Ward

Banana Nut Bread

½ cup butter   1 teaspoon soda
1 cup sugar   2 cups flour
2 eggs   3 bananas, beaten
¼ cup pecans (chopped)

Cream butter and sugar. Add eggs. Mix. Add pecans and bananas and mix together. Add flour and soda. Bake in a greased bundt pan at 350 degrees until done (20-25 minutes).

Virginia O'Keefe Brown

Banana Nut Bread

2 eggs   1 cup pecans
1 cup sugar   ¼ teaspoon salt
1 stick butter   1 scant teaspoon baking soda
3 well ripened bananas   2 cups flour

Separate eggs and beat whites. Place whites in a bowl to one side. Beat the egg yolks. Add sugar, butter and bananas. Beat together until it forms a well mixed thin batter. Add flour, soda, salt and pecans. Add to beaten egg whites. Pour into greased loaf pan and bake 1 hour and 45 minutes at 300 degrees.

Muriel Santa Cruz.

Mexican Cornbread

2 eggs, beaten
1 cup cornmeal
½ cup oil
1 teaspoon salt
¼ cup jalapeno peppers, chopped
6 ounces Cheddar cheese, grated
½ small block Velvetta cheese, melted

1 can cream of corn
1 cup buttermilk
½ teaspoon baking soda
1 onion, chopped

Mix and bake in greased 9x13 pan at 400 degrees for 30 minutes.

Cecilia O'Keefe Neustrom

Rolls (Dinno's)

1½ cups milk
2 tablespoons shortening
1 yeast cake
½ cup warm water
1 tablespoon sugar
4 cups flour
1 egg
1 teaspoon salt

Scald and cool milk. Add shortening. Dissolve yeast in warm water, add sugar and 2 cups of flour and beat well. Add egg, 2 more cups of flour and 1 teaspoon salt. Knead lightly. Let rise two hours. Make into rolls. Let rise ¾ hour. Bake in hot oven (400 degrees) for 15 minutes.

Caroline B. Sasser

Paradise Valley Rolls

1 cup shortening	2 eggs, beaten
¾ cup sugar	1 package yeast
2 teaspoons salt	1 cup warm water
1 cup boiling water	6 cups flour

Pour boiling water over shortening, sugar and salt. Let cool. Beat with electric mixer at low speed, adding eggs, yeast dissolved in a cup of warm water, and flour. Grease the back of a plate and place over the bowl. Refrigerate for several hours.

When ready to make rolls, pinch off a piece of dough and, without kneading, roll it out flat, spread with soft butter and roll it up like a jelly roll. Slice and place each roll into a section of an oiled muffin pan. Let rise for two hours and then bake at 450 degrees for 10 minutes. Dough may be spread with butter, sugar and cinammon for sweet rolls or with a meat spread for cocktail rolls. They will hold in the refrigerator for at least a week.

Maureen O'Keefe Ward

Phifer Cornbread

2 cups corn meal
1 cup pork cracklins
1 teaspoon salt
½ cup sour milk
½ teaspoon soda

Place meal, salt and cracklins in bowl. Pour over enough boiling water to moisten. Add milk and soda. Pour into greased cake pan. Cook one hour in slow oven, at 350 degrees.

Caroline B. Sasser

Mexican Cornbread

1½ cups milk
2 eggs
1 cup corn meal
½ cup flour
1 can cream style corn
¾ cup grated cheese
2 jalapeno peppers chopped fine
¾ cup cooking oil
1 bell pepper chopped fine
1 onion chopped fine
2 teaspoons salt
4 slices bacon
pimento
paprika

Beat eggs in 1 cup milk. Add corn meal, flour, corn, cheese, jalapeno peppers, oil, remaining milk, bell pepper, onion and salt.

Fry bacon in iron skillet. Remove bacon, pour off fat and pour batter in. Crumble bacon on top and lay on strips of pimento. Sprinkle with paprika. Bake at 425 degrees for 40 minutes.

Muriel Santa Cruz

Muriel is the wife of Donald Santa Cruz, vice-president of Gulf National Life Insurance Company. Both Muriel and Donald are cooks par excellence.

Rose Annette O'Keefe

Cajun Cake Squares

1 box yellow cake mix
1 stick butter melted
1 egg, beaten
1 cup chopped pecans

Mix these ingredients together and press into a 9x13 inch pan.

Topping:
1 box powdered sugar
2 beaten eggs
1 8-ounce block cream cheese, softened

Pour topping over mixture and bake at 325 degrees for 40 minutes.

Virginia O'Keefe Brown

CONTRIBUTORS

Among the elder contributors to this cookbook:
Mrs. Teresa O'Keefe, my husband's mother, who is cherished and admired immensely by our family.
Rose M. Brodeur (Moma Rose), my grandmother, and my dearest mother, Cecile B. Saxon (Moma Ces or Ceci) and her sisters, Caroline B. Sasser (Aunt Caro) and Edna Brodeur Key (Aunt Edna) live on in these pages. Through these three ladies the French Canadian influence is felt and enjoyed. Also, Mary Cahill O'Keefe, Nicki C. O'Keefe and Nell Slattery Tierney.

Relatives from my generation contributing:
Rose Annette O'Keefe
Jeremiah Joseph O'Keefe, Sr.
Dr. John B. O'Keefe
Alice Sebastian
Celia Saxon Carron
Myrtle Anne Saxon
Rosemary Slattery Davis
Jo Tierney
Susan Davis Flanagan.

Contributors from my sons, daughters, children-in-law as well as their cousins and grandchildren:
Maureen O'Keefe Ward
Jerry J. "Jody" O'Keefe, Jr.
Annette Longeway O'Keefe
Cecilia O'Keefe Neustrom
Kathryn Ann O'Keefe
Virginia O'Keefe Brown
James Patrick O'Keefe
Janie Barrett O'Keefe
Susan O'Keefe Snyder
Chris Snyder
John Michael O'Keefe, Sr.
Patricia Victoria O'Keefe
Mary O'Keefe Sumrall
Ron Sumrall
Jeffrey Hugh O'Keefe
Justin Bernard O'Keefe
Mercedes O'Keefe Huval
Joseph Saxon O'Keefe
Sam Ward
Justice O'Keefe
Susan Carron

Continued on next page

Friends and neighbors
contributing:
Jennifer Altemus (design
consultant)
Kat Ballou
Andrew Breaux
Myra Breaux
Joe Ann De Gregorio
Gladys Eleuterius
Wanda Fremin
Mercedes Hall
Corita Johnson
Dina Landskroner
Ann Lane

Mary Mahoney
Stephanie Mathews
Lucy Mavar
Deedy Munro
Barbara Neustrom
Florence Pettis
Hazel Pitalo
Susan Pitalo Jordan
Miss Sis Runfalo
Ellen Parks Roche
Muriel Santa Cruz
Florence Savarro
Bernice Simmons
Lorelei Stroble

Joe O'Keefe (c. 1988)

Joe O'Keefe, the youngest of the 13 children in our family, produced and designed *Cooking on the Coast*. Now an editor at *Foreign Affairs* magazine in New York City, he encouraged me and our family to realize this long-deferred dream. His tremendous effort has created a treasure that our family will long cherish.

Rose Annette O'Keefe

Index

Index

Index

Index

Index

COOKING ON THE COAST, INC.
P.O. Box 430
Ocean Springs, MS 39566-0430

Please send _____ copy(ies) of **Cooking on the Coast**   @ $14.95 each _____
Postage and handling   @ $ 2.50 each _____
Mississippi residents add sales tax   @ $ 1.05 each _____
Texas residents add sales tax   @ $ .95 each _____
                                                            TOTAL $ _____

Name _____

Address _____

City _____ State _____ Zip _____

*Make checks or money orders payable to **Cooking On The Coast, Inc.***
(Please allow 4 to 5 weeks for delivery.)

- -

COOKING ON THE COAST, INC.
P.O. Box 430
Ocean Springs, MS 39566-0430

Please send _____ copy(ies) of **Cooking on the Coast**   @ $14.95 each _____
Postage and handling   @ $ 2.50 each _____
Mississippi residents add sales tax   @ $ 1.05 each _____
Texas residents add sales tax   @ $ .95 each _____
                                                            TOTAL $ _____

Name _____

Address _____

City _____ State _____ Zip _____

*Make checks or money orders payable to **Cooking On The Coast, Inc.***
(Please allow 4 to 5 weeks for delivery.)

- -

COOKING ON THE COAST, INC.
P.O. Box 430
Ocean Springs, MS 39566-0430

Please send _____ copy(ies) of **Cooking on the Coast**   @ $14.95 each _____
Postage and handling   @ $ 2.50 each _____
Mississippi residents add sales tax   @ $ 1.05 each _____
Texas residents add sales tax   @ $ .95 each _____
                                                            TOTAL $ _____

Name _____

Address _____

City _____ State _____ Zip _____

*Make checks or money orders payable to **Cooking On The Coast, Inc.***
(Please allow 4 to 5 weeks for delivery.)